MALADETTA.

Pyrenees Central

GÈDRE TO THE GARONNE GAP

A GUIDE TO THE MOUNTAINS FOR WALKERS AND CLIMBERS

Arthur Battagel

GASTONS - WEST COL

PYRENEES CENTRAL

(formerly Pyrenees East)

Gastons West Col Publications
Goring Reading Berks. RG8 9AA

Copyright ©1988 A.T. Battagel
SBN 906227 34 8

Companion volumes:
Pyrenees West
Pyrenees East (formerly Andorra Cerdagne)
Pyrenees High Level Route

Printed in England by
Swindon Press Swindon Wilts.

Contents

INTRODUCTION — 12

General, 12 – Scope of guide, 12 – National parks, 12 – Weather, 13 – Main rock climbing centres, 13 – Geology, 13 – Caving, 14 – Road access, 14 – Parking facilities, 14 – Rail access, 15 – Public transport, 15 – Accommodation, 15 – Huts, 17 – Camping, 23 – Frontier crossing, 23 – Languages, 23 – Equipment, 23 – Mountain rescue, 24 – Historical, 25 – Fauna, 27 – Flora, 28 – Grading of ascents, 28 – Times and distances, 28 – Directions, 28 – Nomenclature, 29

ESTAUBÉ – PINETA – TROUMOUSE — 31

Cirques of Estaubé, Pineta, Troumouse including Monte Perdido

NÉOUVIELLE GROUP — 39

Glère, Packe, Campana de Cloutou, Orédon huts. Pics de Néouvielle, Long, Campbieil, Méchant, Midi de Bigorre, L'Arbizon

VALLÉE D'AURE — 48

Barroude hut and Wall, Vallons de Saux, Moudang, Rioumajou, Port de Cauarère, Pic de Batoua

BARROSA – ORDICETO – SUELZA — 52

Port de Barroude, Ordiceto lake, Puntas Suelza, Fulsa, Trigoniero valley

SOUTHERN LIMESTONE RANGE — 55

Cotiella massif, Peña Montañesa, El Turbón

FRONTIER I — 62

Port de la Pez, Viadós and Soula huts, Gd. Bachimale, Port de Clarabide, Gourgs Blancs, Espingo and Portillon huts. Port d'Oô, Pics des Crabioules, Quayrat, Spijoles, Perdiguère

FRONTIER II — 75

Maupas hut, Pics Lézat, Maupas, Boum. Hospice de France, Port de Venasque, Pic de Sauvegarde

POSETS MASSIF 81

Estós, Viadós, Angel Orús, Clot de Chil (Chia) huts. Pico de Posets, Collardo de Eriste, Gran Pico de Eriste, Agujas de Perramó

MALADETA 91

Renclusa hut, Cregüeña lake, Vallibierna valley, Maladeta summits, Pico de la Maladeta, Pico de Aneto, Tempestades, Margalida, Collado de Salenques, Mulleres group, Pico de la Forcanada, Vallibierna group

ENCANTADOS - AIGÜES TORTES - SANT MAURICI 103

Como lo Forno, Besiberri ridge and hut, Ventosa i Calvell hut, Port de Colomers, Noguera de Tor - Espot, Amitges and Saboredo huts, Agulles d'Amitges, Els Encantats, J.M.Blanch hut, Pics de Peguera, Subenuix

Appendix: Maps and foreign technical publications 117

Index 123

Illustrations

Maladeta	frontis.
Map: Pyrenees Central area	8
Pic Quayrat	22
Monte Perdido	30
Monte Perdido N face diagram	34
Pic de Néouvielle group	38
Map: Estaubé – Pineta – Troumouse – Néouvielle	40
Pic de Néouvielle route diagram	43
Pic Long N face	44
Suelza, Fulsa and Ordiceto lake	53
Map: Vallée d'Aure – Ordiceto	56
Map: Cotiella massif	58
Map: El Turbón	61
Pic Quayrat and Pic Lézat	67
Pic des Spijoles E face	69
New Estós hut	71
Map: Frontier I	72
Seil de la Baque and Pic des Gourgs Blancs	74
Map: Frontier II	76
Pic de Maupas and Pic de Boum	78
Map: Posets massif	82
Angel Orús (Forcau) hut	84
Pico de Posets	86
Map: Maladeta massif	88
Pico de Aneto	95
Aneto from SW route diagram	96
Maladeta massif	98

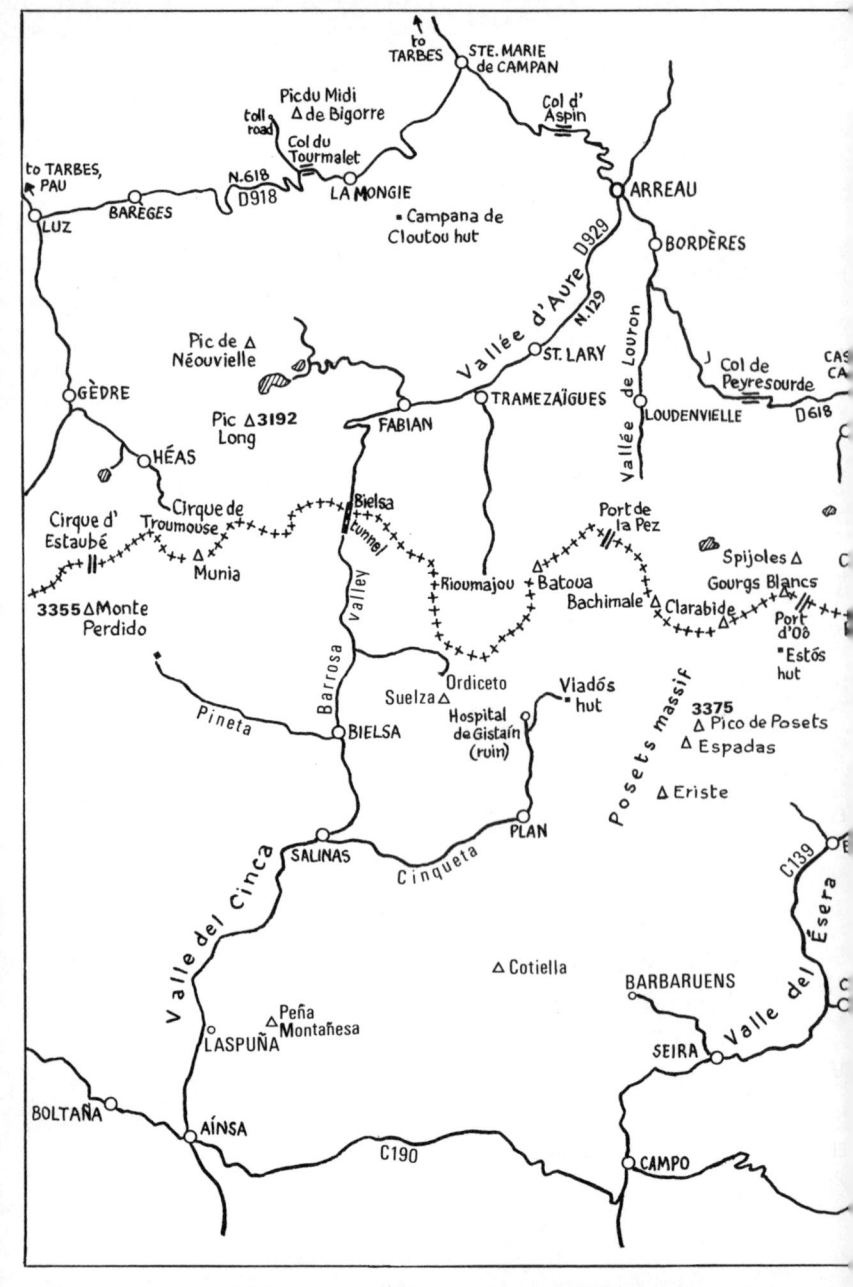

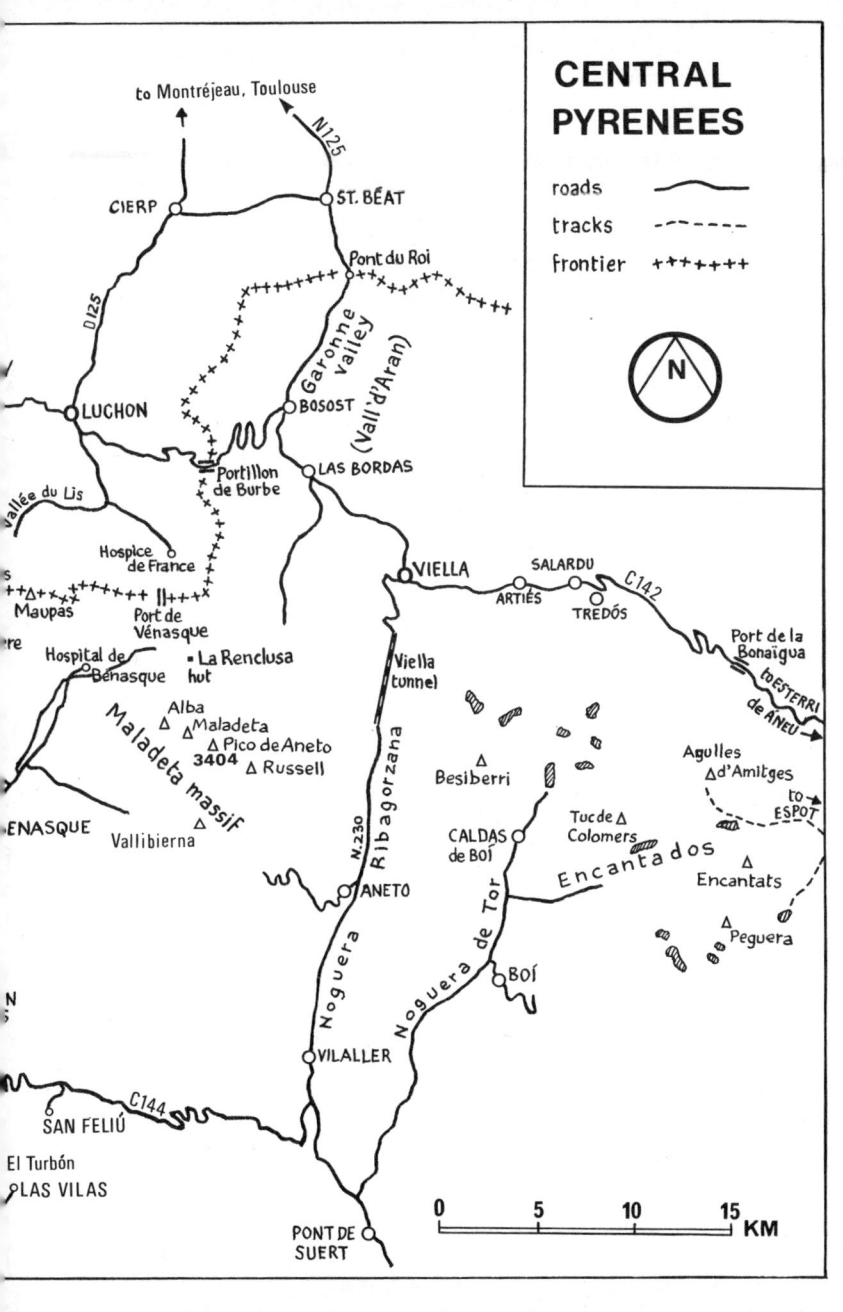

Map: Encantados area	104
Besiberri Nord	108
Serra de Saboredo	111
Els Encantats	113

Photos by: J.M. Sala Albareda, Bernard Clos, X. Gregori, Clive Morgan. Diagrams and drawings by Stephanie Collomb. Other illustrations as stated.

ABBREVIATIONS

br.	bridge
Br.	Brèche (ridge gap)
CAF	French Alpine Club
CEC	Catalonia Excursion Club
EA	Editorial Alpina (maps)
EDF	French national electricity board
FAM	Aragon Mountain Federation
FEEC	Catalonia Mountain Federation
FEM	Spanish Mountain Federation
Fr.	France, French
G	IGN Green tourist map series
Gd(e).	Grand(e)
GR	Long distance trail (n.10, 11)
h.	hour(s)
HRP	Pyrenees High Level Route trail (English code: HP)
ICONA	Spanish forestry service
IGC	Spanish national mapping agency (several variables)
IGN	French national mapping agency
km	kilometres
L	left (direction)
m	metres
m.	against map scale = 1,000, eg. 25m. = 1/25,000 50m. = 1/50,000 etc.
min.	minutes
n.	map sheet or route number
PNP	Pyrenees (French) National Park
pt.	point, map spot height
R	right (direction)
RN	Route nationale (main road)
RP	Randonnées Pyrénéennes Association
SHEM	Mountain hydro-electric board
SNCF	French railways
Sp.	Spain, Spanish
TCF	French Touring Club
V	IGN Violet tourist map series
var.	variation, variant
4WD	4 wheel drive vehicle(s)

compass directions: N, S, E, W, and intermediate directions, eg. NW, SE, etc.

Introduction

GENERAL

Among the mountains of Europe the Pyrenees, both for extent and height, are second only to the Alps. They stretch for some 400 km as a natural frontier between France and Spain and from the Atlantic to the Mediterranean. To those whose experience of mountains has been confined to British hills, the Pyrenees will rank as big mountains. It is fitting that the middle portion of the range offers probably the greatest interest to the mountain traveller.

The area covered by this volume extends from the Cirque d'Estaubé in the W, eastwards along the frontier to the Garonne gap. It includes the Néouvielle group N of the frontier and, in Spain, the large and remote Posets massif and the higher Maladeta, which contains the Pico de Aneto (3404m), the highest summit of the Pyrenees; included also are the Cotiella and the Turbón, far to the S, and the charming lake region of the Aigües Tortes - Encantados. Since the first edition of the guide was issued, 2 new zones in Spain have been added to the present work, and information about walks and climbs has been extended in all other parts.

SCOPE OF GUIDE

In dealing with so extensive an area it is clearly not possible to cover even every simple ascent, let alone every rock climb. Indeed this is not the purpose of the guide. It is merely hoped to give a reasonably balanced picture of the greater part of the area, describing the main massifs and peaks, the huts, routes to them and some of the more interesting scrambles from them. While reference will be made to some of the more important rock climbs, those wishing to attempt them should consult French and Spanish climbing guides - see note at back of book.

NATIONAL PARKS

The 2 cirques of Estaubé and of Troumouse and the southern part of the Néouvielle area lie within the French Pyrenees National Park (PNP). To the N is the older established National Nature Reserve of Néouvielle. In Spain the Aigües Tortes - Sant Maurici National Park covers a large part of the region more generally known as the Encantados. Regulations in these parks about camping are ambiguous, but camping high in the mountains is not restricted.

WEATHER

As this guide covers several large and important areas in Spain, more attention must be given to the weather S of the frontier than need be given for the Western Pyrenees. From mid June to mid September the weather can be relied upon to be good and, in Spain, hot. There will be thunderstorms, usually in the evening or at night, followed by a clear morning.

In the French valleys leading up to the frontier thick clouds frequently rise quickly to the summits during the afternoon and often persist until morning. For this reason an early start for higher expeditions is strongly advised so that the return to the hut or valley can be made by the early afternoon.

MAIN ROCK CLIMBING CENTRES

Though almost all the summits in the area described can be reached without rock climbing proper, this should not be taken to mean that a number of the major peaks do not also provide first class sport for the more advanced rock climber. The main technical climbing areas from W to E are:

a) Barroude Wall.
b) Pic Long (Néouvielle), N face.
c) Quayrat, W and SW faces.
d) Pic des Spijoles, E face.
e) Crabioules, N face.
f) Maupas, S face.
g) Agujas de Perramó - Posets area.
h) Agulles d'Amitges - Encantatos area.

More detailed references to the above and other climbing locations are noted in the text.

GEOLOGY

As in the more western parts of the Pyrenees, the areas described here show a great and confusing variety of rock. The Néouvielle region is granite, as is the high frontier ridge. The Maladeta massif is very mixed, though predominently granite. Further S is the eastern end of the fragmented southern limestone range in the Cotiella and the Turbón, also other outcrops of limestone and schist. The Posets too show a mixture of limestone, schist and granite. In the Encantados area the W and central parts are mainly granite but there is some limestone in the E. As elsewhere in Spain, climbing on compact schist has acquired a certain vogue.

CAVING

In recent years, notably since 1979, considerable exploration has taken place in the Cotiella region in Spain. The EA map booklet for this area lists and gives details of the main caves, which are also shown on the map. The Puerto de Gistaín area at the northern end of the Posets massif also has a number of caves. The name Posets means 'pits', and it is from these caves that the massif takes its name.

ROAD ACCESS

Most visitors from Britain will approach the area from the N. The main towns in the S of France to make for are Tarbes and Bagnères de Luchon, usually known as Luchon. There are 3 road-crossing points from France to Spain: the Bielsa tunnel on the route from Aragnouet in the upper Aure valley to Bielsa in Spain; the Portillon de Burbe between Luchon and Bosost in the Spanish Garonne valley; and the Pont du Roi crossing in the Garonne valley itself. The opening of the Bielsa tunnel, after long delays, has made access to the Posets and Maladeta areas comparatively easy.

In recent years there has been considerable reclassification and re-numbering of roads in France. If older maps are used there may be some confusion. Road numbers given in the guide are revised ones, but older numbers may be cited as well.

Note that from Luchon the minor D.125 going S then SE towards the ancient Hospice de France has been cut by a landslide about 7km from Luchon, just after pt.1240, and there is no early prospect of re-opening the last 2km to the Hospice (1986). A path leads round the land slide to join the road above it.

In Spain 4 main valley roads give access to the principal massifs of the central area: the Cinca valley and its tributary the Cinqueta valley; Ésera valley; Vall d'Aran; and the Noguera Ribagorzana valley. All have important side valleys for inner access, often driveable in small cars. Fuller details are given in the respective districts.

PARKING FACILITIES

There are a few parking areas at roadheads but no guarded parking lots. Normally, locked cars may be left in perfect safety for several days at a time at roadheads or by the roadside where paths leave for huts in both France and Spain. It is clearly advisable to conceal from obvious view items such as transistors, the use of which, incidentally, is strictly forbidden in all club huts.

RAIL ACCESS

In France, as in Britain, many uneconomic branch lines have been shut. Thus the former lines to Bagnères de Bigorre and to Arreau are closed. Although the line to Luchon is still open, the service from Montréjeau Junction is now restricted to one train in each direction in the early morning and in the evening. A railway bus service links these 2 places during the rest of the day. There are no railways in Spain in the area covered by this guide.

PUBLIC TRANSPORT

In France there is a railway bus service from Tarbes via Bagnères de Bigorre to La Mongie on the road from Ste. Marie de Campan to the Col du Tourmalet. Also a railway bus service from Lannemezan on the main Tarbes – Toulouse line to Arreau. From Arreau buses run up the Louron valley to Loudenvielle, the highest village, and up the Aure valley to St. Lary and Fabian. Elsewhere it may be more expedient to take a taxi.

In Spain a bus service operates from Viella through the Viella tunnel and down the Noguera Ribagorzana valley to Pont de Suert, 2km S of the point where the road to Caldas de Boí branches off to the NE. Private local bus services operate in other valleys and taxi hire is easy.

ACCOMMODATION

Troumouse

The Auberge du Maillet is on the toll road to the Cirque de Troumouse. Open 1 July to 1 September.

Aure valley

Arreau – 3 hotels. Cadéac – large expensive hotel in a private park. St. Lary – several hotels, all prices. Rioumajou – the hospice at the roadhead can be used as a shelter for the night; otherwise no services or food available. Shepherds use the building.

Louron valley

Bordères de Louron – good small hotel, moderate prices. Avajan – one small hotel. Estarvielle – small, pleasant hotel on road from Arreau to Col de Peyresourde. Loudenvielle – several small hotels, good.

Larboust valley

Garin – small, old hotel.

Luchon valley

Luchon – many hotels of all categories. Hospice de France – this ancient building has been untenanted for many years and is now in a state of disrepair but open as a hut. No keeper, no food, 15 places.

Lis (Lys) valley

Inn at roadhead, simple, clean and pleasant.

There are hotels also at Luz, Gèdre, Barèges, La Mongie and Ste. Marie de Campan, but these places are generally too distant from the centres of interest to serve as bases.

Pineta valley

At roadhead, State owned Parador 'Monte Perdido'. Luxurious 4 star hotel, expensive; excellent meals more reasonably priced. Some food purchase possible in recent past. Note also hotel may be closed at times in the summer.

Cinca valley

Bielsa – several small inns.   Salinas – new hotel.

Cinqueta valley   Plan – inns.

Ésera valley

Castejón de Sos – small hotel. Eriste – 2 small hotels. Benasque – a variety of new hotels; inns. This resort is in process of rapid development.

Vall d'Aran

Viella – large Parador on road from town to the Viella tunnel; also 5 2-star hotels.

Viella – Esterri de Aneu road

Artiés – Hosteria Nacional de Tourismo, pleasant State hotel.
Salardu – pleasant hotel, moderate prices. Baqueira-Beret ski resort – several hotels, some open in summer.
Los Abetos – on road between Port de Bonaigua and Esterri – a modern, pleasant hotel.

Noguera Ribagorzana valley

Hospital de Viella – at S end of the Viella tunnel, old municipal inn.

Open from May to December, very rough; has several beds and sometimes food.

Noguera de Tor valley

Boí - 3 small hotels. Caldas de Boi - 2 hotels in private gardens (4- and 2-star respectively); inns.

Escrita valley

Espot - several hotels/inns, including 2-star and 1-star.

HUTS

France

Handbooks are published in France and Spain purporting to list all huts in the Pyrenees, complete with basic access details and facilities/ amenities provided. This kind of information tends to go out of date quickly. The numerous huts of the French Alpine Club (CAF) all have hut-keepers unless otherwise stated. The reduced price for CAF members and members of reciprocating alpine clubs of other countries rises annually, like most other services, and in 1987 was about £4 for dormitory accommodation. Non members pay double. Huts with keepers provide a meals service (not cheap), and prices are the same for every one. Self-catering is usually possible.

The PNP Authority has built a number of pleasant huts designed and sited for the walker rather than the climber. Charges are similar to CAF huts; also other services. The RP Association has opened a number of Gîtes d'Étapes - well appointed but simple huts for walkers. These have no hut-keepers and do not provide food; a hut-minder, to whom payment is made, lives nearby. RP huts provide bunks, blankets, toilet facilities, stoves and cooking utensils with accommodation for about 15 persons. Dates of opening given below are subject to alteration if heavy snow persists.

Cirque d'Estaubé

Tuquerouye hut   2666m
The first CAF hut in the Pyrenees, built in 1890, in the Br. de Tuquerouye on the frontier. No hut-keeper. It now consists of 2 small biv. shells with spartan accommodation for 20. It has been due for re-building for many years. For approaches, see Estaubé section.

Néouvielle district

Orédon hut/inn 1852m
Aragnouet commune (formerly TCF). Above the E end of the Orédon lake, reached by a short side road from the new road to Lac d'Aubert. A simple hotel rather than a hut. Full meal service, moderate prices, 35 places.

Oule chalet/hotel 1819m
Beneath the dam of the Lac d'Oule. Reached by a path (2km) from Artigusse (parking) on the Fabian - Cap de Long road, D.929. Simple restaurant service, 30 places, open 15 June to 30 September.

Glère hut/hotel 2120m
More a hotel, situated about halfway between the Barèges - Tourmalet col road and the Lac d'Aubert. Now accessible by road, but probably closed to private vehicles. Full service, heating and showers, about 90 places, open 1 July to 30 September.

Packe hut 2509m
CAF. Named after the 19th century pioneer, Charles Packe. Door open, no hut-keeper, old and small though somewhat improved during the 1970s. Places for 8 with blankets and mattresses.

Campana de Cloutou hut 2225m
CAF. Burnt down in 1979 and rebuilt. Warden usually resident, 25 places, blankets, some kitchen equipment and gas burner.

For routes to the above huts, see Néouvielle section.

Vallée d'Aure

Vielle-Aure Gîte d'étape 800m
RP. In Vielle-Aure village on side road to W of main Aure valley road. 16 places, open all year.

Aulon Gîte d'étape 1250m
RP. In Aulon village at end of road 4km SW of Guchen village in the Aure valley. 15 places, open all year.

Barroude hut 2373m
PNP. Beneath the Barroude Wall. Warden in summer, simple meals service, 20 places, open 1 July to 15 September. For route to hut, see Vallée d'Aure section.

Clarabide valley

Soula hut 1700m
SHEM. Not a hut proper; located in one of the Electricity Board's buildings at La Soula power station. Full meal service, hot water

and electric heating, good, plentiful food at moderate prices, 40/50 places, open 1 June to mid September. For route, see Frontier I.

Caillauas hut 2171m
SNCF. No keeper or facilities, about 10 places.

Pouchergues hut 2111m
At the Lac de Pouchergues. No keeper or facilities, about 12 places.

Arrouge - Astau valleys

Lac d'Oô hut/inn 1504m
Full services, 30 places, open 15 June to 10 October.

Espingo hut 1967m
CAF. Hut keeper and restaurant service, 80 places, open 15 June to 30 September. For route, see Frontier I section.

Portillon hut 2570m
CAF. At the Lac du Portillon. Warden, simple meals service, places for 45, open 1 July to 15 September. See Frontier I section.

Lis (Lys) valley

Maupas hut 2430m
CAF. Hut keeper, simple meals service, 40 places, open 1 July to 15 September. See Frontier II section.

Pique valley

Venasque hut 2239m
CAF. No hut-keeper, door open, 12 places, equipment inventory doubtful. On the path from the Hospice de France to the Port de Venasque. See Frontier II section.

Spain

Though the important Maladeta massif is rather poorly served, most of the other Sp. districts now have numerous though small huts. Dates of opening given below are subject to alteration is heavy snow persists.

Trigoniero valley

Trigoniero hut 1970m
ICONA. Small forestry hut with no facilities, situated S of the Port du Moudang. See Vallée d'Aure and Barrosa sections.

Cotiella massif

Armeña hut   1860m
FAM. In the Armeña cirque on E side of the massif. Reached from roadhead at Barbaruens village and forest track. New in 1980, hut-keeper occasionally present, full kitchen inventory, 25/30 places. See Southern Limestone Range section.

Cinqueta valley

Viadós hut   1760/1810m
Although privately owned this hut is open to all. Full meal service, open 1 July to 15 September. For routes, see Frontier II and Posets sections.   40 places.

Tabernés hut   1700m
ICONA forestry hut, open to all, close to the Viadós hut and consequently not very useful.

Estós valley

Estós hut   1835m
FEM. Old hut destroyed in 1979. New hut opened 1985. Full meal service, self cooking room, 200 places. For approaches, see Frontier II and Posets sections. Open all the year.

Ésera valley

Renclusa hut   2140m
CEC. Warden and staff, full meal service, 110 places. Usually crowded, so early arrival is advised. There is also a small, old and rather squalid annexe. Open 1 July to 24 September. For routes, see Frontier II and Maladeta sections.

Angel Orús (Forcau) hut   2095m
FEM. Built in 1981; hut-keeper, simple meals, 40 places. On track from Eriste to Posets massif (qv).

Clot de Chil (Chia)   1980/1990m
FEM/ICONA. An open forestry hut; serves the Ixea/Perramó groups of the Posets massif (qv).

Encantados

Besiberri biv. hut   2760/2820m
FEEC. Found just below the crest of the Besiberri NE ridge. No hut-keeper, 12 places, gas cooker and small food store for emergencies only. See Besiberri Nord.

Joan Ventosa i Calvell hut   2220m
CEC. Above the Estany Negre, NE of the Cavallers lake. Rebuilt in 1979, hut-keeper during summer, restaurant service, 80 places. An Electricity Board hut nearby can also be used.

Restanca hut   2010m
FEEC. Piste road to within 30 min. of hut. Hut-keeper occasionally present during summer; otherwise key should be obtainable at a nearby hut belonging to the Electricity Board, which will be seen at the other end of the dam of the Restanca lake. Equipment inventory complete, 26 places.

Colomers hut   2086m
FEEC. On the banks of the Estany Major de Colomers in the N of the region; piste road approach to within 45 min. walk. Door open, summary equipment, generally no warden, 20 places.

Estany Llong hut   1985m
At the head of the Sant Nicolau valley. Now closed.

Saboredo hut   2200m
FEEC. To the N of the region. No hut-keeper, summary equipment, 20 places.

Amitges hut   2380m
CEC. One of the best huts in the area. Warden, restaurant service, 56 places. Open 1 July to 30 September and during weekends in October. 4WD vehicle access.

Ernest Mallafre hut   1930m
FEEC. Near the Sant Maurici lake dam. Hut keeper, 18 places in beds, simple meal service. Best base for the Encantats.

J.M. Blanch hut   2350m
FEEC. At the Estany Tort, SW of Espot. Hut-keeper, some food and drink, 36 places, open throughout the year. Accessible in 4WD vehicles.

Colomina hut   2395m
FEEC. On the banks of the Estany Colomina, SW of the Blanch hut. 20 places. Often no hut-keeper; keys obtainable from the FEEC in Barcelona. However, the hut is now frequently wardened in summer.

Vall d'Aran

Chalet Juli Soler i Santaló   1268m
CEC. On the main road at Salardu. All services, 105 places, open throughout the year.

Pic Quayrat from the Portillon d'Oô.

CAMPING

Camping is officially prohibited within the area of the Pyrenees National Park, France, and also within the Aigues Tortes - Sant Maurici National Park, Spain. In spite of notices to this effect, there appears to be no objection to individual tents being pitched for they are to be seen in fair numbers in both these parks. Otherwise you may camp on the mountains where you wish. There are official camping areas in the lower inhabited valleys, normally marked on tourist topographical maps.

FRONTIER CROSSING

At the road frontier crossing points of the Bielsa tunnel, Portillon de Burbe and Pont du Roi, the usual formalities are observed. In 1967 an agreement was made between the French and Spanish authorities allowing free passage of the frontier on foot by any route to all holders of a special card issuable by recognised alpine clubs to its members. This applies to entry to the Spanish Province of Huesca, which means, on the Fr. side, the whole of the frontier covered in this guide W of the Garonne gap watershed and the valley of the Noguera Ribagorzana. The CAF issues such cards to its members but, in practice, since 1967 mountain travellers have never been challenged in Spain and asked for such a card. It seems that the Spanish frontier guards use their common sense in recognising bona fide climbers and walkers. The French, since 1968, as indeed before, appear to be quite unconcerned by casual frontier crossing.

LANGUAGES

A working knowledge of French or Spanish is useful. English is not generally understood, except in larger hotels in tourist centres. In the huts, a few people may be met by chance who can help. French is understood and spoken to some extent on the Sp. side of the frontier and vice versa. In Spain, the normal everyday language in the Province of Huesca is the Aragonese dialect. In the Province of Lérida, E of the Noguera Ribagorzana, the language is Catalan, though standard Castillian Spanish is also spoken in both provinces.

EQUIPMENT

What you should take depends on what you intend to do. The minimum for the least ambitious mountain walker should include good mountain boots with Vibram or similar soles, hooded water and windproof anorak, heavy and light sweater, breeches and heavy woollen stockings and a woollen cap. A torch and spare batteries should also be carried; useful

in unlighted hut dormitories as well as for signalling in case of trouble.
Large scale maps of the area are essential and a compass can be useful.
Although most huts provide blankets, a lightweight sleeping bag is recommended. For those intending more than walking, full alpine gear
should be taken. Ice axes are useful on many of the routes to the higher peaks and some of the less easy scrambles require a rope. Although
crampons are not generally necessary, there are some routes in this area
where they can be advantageous in certain conditions. Glaciers are of
the cirque variety, ie. breadth without length. They lie under some
of the higher crests and ridges and are snow covered in summer. Though
some are quite heavily crevassed, in normal summers crevasses are well
covered and present no problem. Those intending to rock climb will
need no advice.

MOUNTAIN RESCUE

This is well organised on the French side. The Mountain Rescue Service has all the usual equipment for high altitude work, including helicopters that also carry out routine patrols. Do not call out the rescue
service unless it is absolutely essential. Apart from involving a lot of
people in possibly unnecessary work, it will prove extremely expensive.
When reporting an accident with which the party cannot cope, the
messenger should mark the exact spot of the injured person on the map
and take it to the nearest hut or nearest inhabited valley, whichever
is the closer in terms of time. The marking of the map can be important. The messenger may have language or other difficulties in giving
the exact location of the injured person and he is likely to be too tired
to act as a guide to the rescue team, who will wish to set a pace too
fast for him.

All huts with keepers hold a certain amount of rescue equipment and,
in France, are equipped with radio receiver-transmitters in touch with
the Gendarmerie; radio communications are now also good in the main
Spanish huts. Search for a phone in a valley may be a long job but,
once found, the Gendarmerie should be asked for in France and the
Guardia Civil in Spain. Unless you are fluent in Fr. or Sp. do not
try to give details over the phone. Say simply that there has been an
accident and where you are phoning from and wait for their arrival,
when you can show the marked map and give details of the injuries.
The French service in action impresses with speed and efficiency. The
author has no personal knowledge of the service in Spain. Rescue
equipment is kept in all the larger Spanish huts, and in the Encantados most of these can be reached by 4WD vehicles.

Visitors should insure themselves against the potential high cost of mountain rescue; easy to arrange and comparatively cheap in Britain.

HISTORICAL

The valleys of the Pyrenees have been inhabited from the earliest times, but it was not until the end of the 18th century that any serious attempt was made to explore the mountains themselves. The local people seem to have known only their own valleys, though shepherds and hunters knew something of the heights. It was not the local people however, but outsiders, who started to explore.

Nevertheless a few eccentrics were attracted by the peaks long before the 18th century. There was, for instance, Pedro III of Aragon who in 1280 claimed to have reached the summit of the Canigou where, so he said, he and his companions had disturbed a dragon they found living in a lake. It would, perhaps, be safer to place this monarch's ascent in the category of legend.

But the first great name is that of Louis-François Ramond who came to Barèges by chance in 1787. A man interested in the natural sciences, he explored not for fun but in pursuit of knowledge. Although he spent only 5 weeks in the Pyrenees in 1787, he made a long journey from Barèges and crossed the frontier by the Port d'Oô at 2908m - to which there was already a track marked by cairns - and went down into the Estós valley and on to Benasque. He made the first recorded ascent to the Maladeta summit ridge, very probably at the Collado de Alba of over 3000m. He returned to the Pyrenees in 1792 for a stay of eight weeks but never again travelled very far from Barèges or Bagnères de Bigorre, except for his visits to the Br. de Tuquerouye, Mte. Perdido and the Ordesa valley.

Exploration moved slowly during the first half of the 19th century; but the Pico de Aneto was climbed in 1842 by a Frenchman, Albert de Franqueville, and a Russian, Platon Chihachev, and 4 local men. At that time climbing on snow was disliked and the party did not take the easy route across the Aneto glacier but a long and complicated one, reaching the summit from the SW.

In 1856 Halkett reached the summit of the second highest mountain of the Pyrenees, the Pico de Posets.

Then in 1861 Count Henry Russell began a Pyrenean campaign, which was to last 43 years. Born in Toulouse, but of Irish descent, he was a romantic and an eccentric. Very few summits were left unvisited by him, many being first ascents, during his long career. Though famous for his devotion to the Vignemale in the Western Pyrenees, he did much exploration in the Maladeta and Posets massifs and on the high frontier tops. He covered prodigious distances day after day, slept out on the open mountainside in his sheepskin sleeping bag in all weathers, and disliked the idea of huts. Going up to see the new Tuquerouye hut in 1891 he gave it little prospect of survival in so exposed a position, but it remained until a few years ago. To travel in the Posets area at this time was adventurous indeed. Once, on the western slopes of this massif, he had a night encounter with a band of armed brigands. His most permanent memorial is his great mountaineering classic "Souvenirs d'un Montagnard", now very difficult to find.

Linked with Russell is his friend Charles Packe, a Leicestershire land owner and a botanist. Packe did much pioneer work in the great Spanish massifs, regions all but unknown at the time. In 1862 he published his "Guide to the Pyrenees", the first to appear in English. 4 years later he produced the first, and remarkably accurate, map of the Maladeta massif based on his own observations. Though not an eccentric in the manner of Russell, Packe had his idiosyncracies. For several years he was accompanied by 2 great Pyrenean dogs, which followed him to the summits. Also, so Russell tells us, he became intensely irritated if anyone mentioned "feet" to him when speaking of heights; he thought and spoke in "metres" only, surely an oddity for an Englishman at the time. He is commemorated by the Estany Packe, a tarn at the foot of the Pico Russell (Maladeta), as well as by the hut that bears his name.

Both Russell and Packe were content to find the easiest routes to their summits but there were other more adventurous spirits in the field. Thus Roger de Monts who, in 1879, made the first winter ascent of the Aneto and, in the following winter, reached the summit of the Posets.

It was at the turn of the century that a new team of 5 young men came upon the scene, astonishing their contemporaries by the audacity of their exploits. These were the Cadier brothers from Osse, a village in the Aspe valley in the Western Pyrenees. Though the majority of the new and difficult routes they opened lie in the western districts, the eldest of the brothers, George, on their first visit to the Maladeta massif, forced a new route up the N rockface of the Pico de Tempestades, a summit on the ridge SE of the Aneto.

During the inter-war years Dr Jean Arlaud was, perhaps, the most brilliant virtuoso climber in the Pyrenees. He opened a very large number of extremely difficult routes, especially on the high frontier ridge and also in the Maladeta and Posets massifs. His career was brought to an early close by a fall from a ridge on the Gourgs Blancs in 1938.

In the last 50 years the number of first class climbers, both French and Spanish, has increased rapidly. New and more difficulty routes are still being opened and repeated as winter climbs. Spaniards came late into the field of mountain exploration; even in Spain pioneer work was left almost exclusively to the French and indeed, until as recently as 20 years ago, relatively few Spaniards were to be met; hardly any on the Fr. side of the frontier. Now, however, they are making a strong contribution to the development of more difficult routes.

FAUNA

A brief note on the more interesting species. Pride of place must be given to the Isard, the chamois of the Pyrenees. It is slightly smaller than the chamois of the Alps and can be seen fairly frequently at a distance, grazing round about the snow line in summer. They are not easy to pick out among the rocks.

There are supposed to be about 50 bears left in the Pyrenees. This is the large European Brown Bear. The author has never seen one. They live on the low forest slopes and are said to make off smartly, deeper into the forest at the approach of man.

Marmots are not native to the Pyrenees but during the last 30 years several colonies have been introduced from the Alps. These are now well established but their numbers are still comparaively small. The author has seen them only once, in the Néouvielle district.

The wild boar is to be found in the Encantados region, but the rarest of Pyrenean mammals is the curious Desman, a creature about the size of a large rat with a pointed snout and half-webbed feet. It lives in the banks of streams and outside the Pyrenees is found only in the Caucasus.

In spite of persistent but vague rumours, it had long been thought that the Ibex or Bouquetin had been shot out of existence. Fairly recently, however, a sighting by an entirely reliable observer has been reported. This is unlikely to be confirmation of survival, for the ibex is to be found in other parts of Spain and it may, perhaps, be assumed that the specimen had found its way into the Pyrenees.

Even though the Golden Eagle is still to be found, any large bird seen circling is far more likely to be a Griffin Vulture. It has been estimated that there are no more than a few dozen of these vultures in the whole range; all but a few may be seen together whenever a dead sheep is discovered in the high pastures. This great bird can be seen often at close range and is easily distinguished by its white neck ruff and bare pink neck.

The small Egyptian Vulture is a summer visitor. Not as common as the Griffin, it can be seen occasionally. It has an orange-yellow head and from below appears white. The third and most rare is the Lammergeyer or Bearded Vulture, distinguished in flight by the silhouette of its tail.

FLORA

One need not be a botanist to realise and enjoy the great variety of flowers, both in the valleys and on the heights in the Pyrenees. One of the most vivid memories from the author's first visit is of the sea of blue and yellow iris covering the pastures of the upper Gállego valley in the Western Pyrenees. Another is from the pastures at the head of the Ordesa canyon, where one morning in mid July the air was thick with the scent of dark rich honey. All who climb to the summits will see the gentians as they pass without, perhaps, distinguishing between the different varieties. The botanist will know that the Pyrenees offer one of the richest fields in Europe for his search for rare specimens, and will make several visits at different times of the year between late April and the end of September.

GRADING OF ASCENTS

These are based on the international system for general mountaineering and rock climbing, as translated from the French. In rising order of seriousness and difficulty the general application is: F, PD, AD, D, TD, ED, etc. The numerical equivalent for strictly rock pitches is: I, II, III, IV, V, VI, etc. Both are qualified for more accuracy by plus (+) or minus (-) signs to indicate high or low in the grade. Many routes in this guide, including most hut walks, etc. are labelled 'Ungraded'. Elsewhere in Europe this category is defined as 'elementary' or for 'pedestrians' and is shown by the letters E or P. Traditionally F used to cover this category, but the tendency nowadays is to divorce mountaineering standards from walking and scrambling ones. In general there are no detailed route descriptions above the level of AD+ (III+) in this guide. In British rock climbing parlance this is equivalent to the traditional 'very difficult' grade. F would be equivalent to Bristly Ridge in Snowdonia or Striding Edge on Helvellyn.

TIMES AND DISTANCES

Times are very relative, depending on the age, ability and fitness of the walker. PNP signposts give times to places indicated but tend to be erratic in over and under estimates by a wide margin. Times given will tend to err on the long side; no allowance is made for halts and distances are given in kilometres (km) only.

LEFT AND RIGHT

(L, R). Unless otherwise indicated, when used with reference to the bank or side of a stream, L and R mean in the direction in which you are moving, up or down, and not as previously stated in relation to the downward flow of the stream. This rule may also apply to other features. Eg. where formerly you went up the L bank of a gully (in reality the R side in ascent), you now go up the R side; and in descent you come down the L side.

NOMENCLATURE

As the frontier runs through many of the summits, these often have both French and Spanish names. Most of these are similar enough to avoid confusion. Because much of the early exploration in Spain was done by Frenchmen, some of the purely Spanish peaks are better known by their French names; eg Monte Perdido is more usually known as Mont Perdu. In such cases both versions are given. Many topographical features have names in the local language. IGN has 'frenchified' them on some maps, giving a standard French rendering which approximates to the local pronunciation. Some recent maps have reverted to local spellings. Similar chopping and changing occurs on the Spanish side of the frontier. In the Encantados region there are 3 or more spellings of nearly all mountain names; maps vary wildly in this respect but there should be no difficulty identifying names in the guide which may be written differently on some maps.

Monte Perdido. NE face and Pineta lake (Lac Glacé) from the Brèche de Tuquerouye.

Estaubé - Pineta - Troumouse

Maps: IGN 50m. n.1748. IGN/RP 50m. n.4. IGN 25m. V n.275, 276. EA 40m. n.204, 25m. n.205.   IGN 25m. DB n.1748W.

Cirque d'Estaubé

This lies at the head of a short valley immediately E of the Gave de Pau valley and the Gavarnie cirque. The Troumouse cirque lies to the E again of the Estaubé. Both cirques are reached by a road from Gèdre, in the Gave de Pau valley, that runs up the Gave de Héas valley. About 6km up this valley a short road forks R and climbs to the Gloriettes dam, which is at the entrance of the Gave d'Estaubé, extending for another 6km.

Brèche de Tuquerouye   2666m

Sp. Tucarroya. Grade, PD (crampons). This famous frontier pass was first crossed by Ramond in 1797. The N face of Monte Perdido fills the scene to the S. At that time and well into the 19th century this face was adorned by an icefall of some dimensions that impressed all who saw it. It has now completely disappeared.

From the roadhead (D.176) at the Gloriettes dam (1668m), cross dam: the Perdido summit is seen at the head of the valley above the Brèche. Follow path (HRP) round N end of lake and along its W bank. Do not cross the stream by a footbridge 2km S of the lake but follow the big HRP track that, on approaching the head of the valley (the cirque), starts to climb the western slopes to the Hourquette d'Alans. At pt.2232 take a lesser fork L, which, following the contour, curves SE round the cirque. After about one km fork R on a minor track marked by cairns and climb towards a prominent isolated sugar-loaf of rock, the Borne de Tuquerouye. Climb above the Borne (2471m) and reach a wide gully on its R side which leads to the Tuquerouye gap. This fairly steep couloir, broad at its foot and narrowing appreciably towards the top, can be tricky and slow in adverse conditions. It is usually filled with frozen snow but conditions vary considerably and late in the season the upper half may be transformed into ice, when crampons are essential. Ascend gully for 200m, keeping to the W side, and reach the Tuquerouye hut in the pass itself. The view of Perdido is worth the effort ($3\frac{1}{2}$-$4\frac{1}{2}$ h.). Originally, Ramond climbed the gully in 2h. using primitive crampons; but a month later, when the party found ice, his time was 5h.

Circo de Pineta

From Bielsa (1053m) the Pineta valley extends WNW for 14km to a roadhead (1280m) at the Mte. Perdido Parador and a small chapel; taxis from Bielsa. Carpark in front of hotel; a footbridge opposite crosses the wide river (boulders and several streams in summer) to an area on the far side for discretionary camping; further up on this side is a tiny forestry hut. Note that this hotel has an erratic record of being open and closed; some simple food purchase possible in the past.

At the roadhead a path continues along the N side of the main stream, rising gradually WNW for about 2 km to c. 1700m. Here it starts rising steeply, winding up for another 2km and crossing 3 or 4 minor streams to emerge with a circular movement S in the cirque at 2500m. The path contours in the same WNW direction as the Balcón de Pineta, towards ruined barns, and from there slants a short way N to meet the Tuquerouye hut - Cuello de Cilindro path coming N-S along the W shore of the Pineta lake (2590m). This picturesque lake site (floating ice to mid season) has been given at least 4 different names (though 6 can be traced); in adopting Pineta we elect the most obvious which cannot be confused with any other name. Superb view of the snowy NE flanks of Perdido - Cilindro - Marboré ($4\frac{1}{2}$-5h.).

From the N corner of the lake climb boulders further R, but L of gully line beneath the Tuquerouye gap, to about 30m. below the skyline; go R along a ledge into the gully and climb it over blocks to hut in gap at the top (20 min.).

Pineta - Estaubé cirque connection by the Port Neuf de Pinède (2466m)

This route has historical significance in that Ramond returned this way from his first visit to the Pineta lake in 1797. Today it is not really recommended, although it looks deceptively shorter (and easier) than going over the Br. de Tuquerouye. At c. 1840m on the path from the Parador to the Pineta cirque, a vague track branches NNE but fades out some distance from the Port Neuf, where the terrain becomes quite difficult. However, on the Fr. side of the pass an easy path slants W below the Estaubé headwall to join the regular Fr. route to the Tuquerouye hut/gap below the Borne.

Pic de Pinède   2860m

The imposing headwall of the Estaubé cirque is filled by a serrated rock ridge with the Pinède as its centrepiece. Its complete traverse, from the Port Neuf (2466m), over the Pte. du Forcarral (2717m) to the Tuquerouye gap is one of the limestone ridge testpieces of the Central area, on account of the atrocious rock in sensational positions; some pitches of IV and V. The long, tame-looking section between the Pinède top and the Tuquerouye gap is III+.

MONTE PERDIDO 3355m

Fr. Mont Perdu. Misprinted 3335 on IGN/RP map 1985 Ed. Together with the Cilindro and Ramond, collectively grouped in Spain as Las Tres Sorores (= hermanas = sisters). The third highest peak in the Pyrenees. It is massive and while having no great rock faces the N/NE (Pineta) side has interesting snowy climbs. The southern (Ordesa) approach to the normal route, taken by most visitors, is described in the companion volume, Pyrenees West.

Southern Route approached from North via Cuello de Cilindro   Grade, PD.

From the Tuquerouye hut drop S down a gully of boulders for c.25-30m, move R(W) along a ledge then descend a boulder slope to the W end of the Pineta lake (see Pineta cirque, above). Now follow cairned track S across shelving floor of cirque (snow) and climb to the foot of a gully in a long low rockband. Go up this and move R across a terrace to a second and steeper gully slanting L in rocks above. Climb this and go over snow slopes to the Cuello de Cilindro (3070m), an obvious wide saddle. From this pass descend to a rock ledge and follow it R for a short way before dropping down on boulders to the Lago Hélado where the normal route from the Delgado/Goriz hut is joined at c.2985m in $2\frac{1}{2}$h.

Now ascend snow SE, on the L(N) side of a low rock ridge falling from the visible summit of Perdido. Continue beside this subsidiary ridge, in a broad couloir, until the route bears round steeply to the L under a rock band and into a broad gully (snow). At the head of this, climb a short steep bar of boulders to the R and so reach snow slopes below the summit cone. Bear L and rise in a curve to the top, reaching it from the N; about $1\frac{1}{2}$h. from Hélado tarn, 4h. from Tuquerouye hut.

North-West Ridge   Grade, PD.

A good climb. Go to the Cilindro saddle as for the previous route from the Tuquerouye ($2\frac{1}{4}$h.). Start up the broad ridge on boulders and snow; keep to the spine as far as a gap dominated by a squat gendarme called Dedo (Fr. Doigt, 3188m). Turn this on the L(N) side over steep snow slopes at its base, and reach a gully rising to the crest again.   Climb the now steeper and narrower ridge, initially slightly on the L side, on the R side higher up, and finish directly by the crest at the summit ($1\frac{1}{4}$h, $3\frac{1}{2}$h. from hut).

MONTE PERDIDO N face

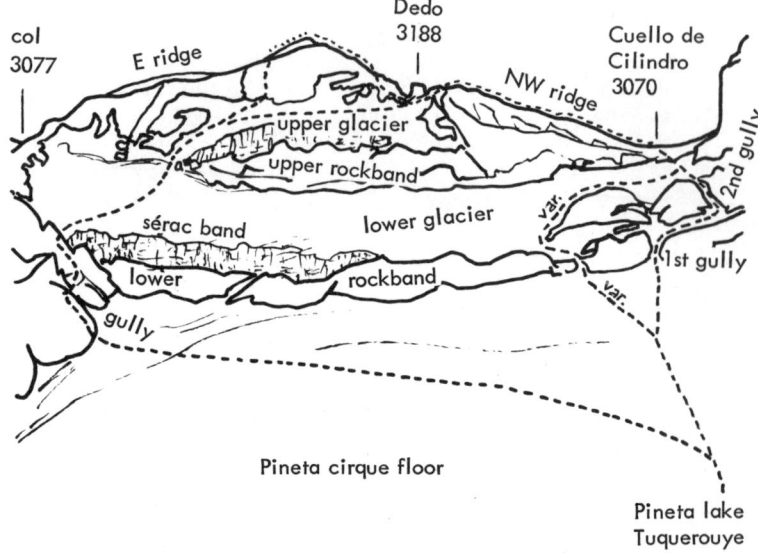

North Face   Grade, AD.   Axe, crampons, etc.

First climbed over 100 years ago, and then rated as the finest ice route in the Pyrenees. Steady regression of the glaciers has made the climb much easier, but it is still subject to variations in the amount of snow cover, both annually and seasonally. Though slightly pretentious by modern standards, an excellent mixed mountaineering route.

Follow the usual way towards the Cilindro saddle (above); on nearing the first gully in the lower rockband, traverse L(SE) across steep rubble (snow) some distance below it, towards the L end in a corner.   This rockband supports a bar of séracs forming the snout of the lower Perdido glacier; serious danger from falling ice all along, right into the corner. Cross snow to the first major inlet gully L of the corner; the danger is now minimised. Climb rocks on L side of this (II) to a scree or snow hollow above the lower gully; traverse R on to a pillar/buttress further R and climb this on polished rocks (III) to exit R at the extreme L end of the sérac band. Go across the moderately inclined glacier to a bergschrund under a steep snow/ice and rock inlet slanting

R above a big rock barrier to the upper glacier. Cross the bergschrund (sometimes large) and climb diagonally R at 50° to the upper glacier. Trend up steeply L across the R end of a tributary glacier band (schrund) to gain rocks under the E ridge, somewhat to the R of a shallow depression. Go up a narrow gully, merging into smooth slabby rock (II/III) and finish on the E ridge not far from the summit.

An easier finish traverses over the upper glacier to reach the couloir going up to the NW ridge beyond the Dedo gendarme (see above). For either way, allow 5-6h. from Tuquerouye hut.

Note: The summits of the Cilindro, Marboré and the Astazou peaks, also encompassed round the Pineta cirque, are described in the West volume guidebook.

Cirque de Troumouse

The largest true cirque in the Pyrenees, 4km in diameter, and formed by three-quarters of a circle of almost level mountain wall. The road from Gèdre passes by the hamlet of Héas and the Héas chapel, then ascends in zigzags to the extensive floor of the cirque (2100m). The whole of the road from the chapel to the terminus is now a toll byway. The main summits round the cirque wall, from E to W, are: Pic de Gerbats (2904m), Pic Heid (3022m), Pic de Troumouse (3085m), Pic de la Munia (3133m) and Pène Blanque (2905m).

PIC DE LA MUNIA 3133m

IGC 3134m. More difficult and longer from the Sp. side. The highest point on the Troumouse cirque wall. Grade, PD. From carpark at end of toll road cross pastures ESE which form the floor of the cirque, on a heading slightly W of the summit line. There are various tracks but, on reaching boulder slopes at the wall foot, follow a track in the rocks eastwards, passing a promising gully and reaching a second one, usually snow filled, which rises SW. The foot of this gully is at the figure 8 of pt.2418 on map n.276. The gully is steep and early in the morning the frozen snow needs crampons for comfort. Climb the gully keeping under the R-hand wall; at the top bear L and pass under a thin waterfall. The route then bears half R and climbs an easy semi-chimney. At the top turn L and climb an easy rock terrace to the foot of a fairly long snow slope, rising gently to the frontier saddle of the Col de la Munia (2853m). Monte Perdido and the Sum de Ramond are seen to the SW.

From the saddle turn L up the W ridge. The route is fairly clear, in most places just below the crest on the N side. Only in one place,

marked by cairns, does the route double back, on the N side, to reach
the crest again. After this a short inclined slab, the Pas de Chat, is
reached. This pitch is split from top to bottom by 2 narrow cracks (II)
with good holds. Above, continue on the crest, across the heads of 2
gullies and, by broken rock, attain the summit. About $3\frac{1}{2}$h. from the
carpark. The view is very fine, comprising the Vignemale in the W,
all the Gavarnie peaks, Monte Perdido, the Néouvielle summits to
the N, and the Posets massif to the E.

Troumouse Cirque Ridge Traverse   Grade, PD+.

A classic Pyrenees Central rock scramble, long and demanding certain
experience. An obvious shorter version is popular, starting by the Munia normal route (above) to reach the ridge at the Munia col.

From the roadhead carpark, ascend slopes SW and enter a broad gully
between 2 triangular spur-ends, pts.2606 and 2597 (Tumeu de Bouneu).
Climb the gully by steep slopes of slate and shifting scree with snow
patches and reach the frontier ridge at the Port de la Canau (2620m).
Fine view S down into the Pineta valley.

Turn E along a track on the frontier ridge, very narrow with steep
slopes on both sides, and reach the Pic de Bouneu (2726m). Here the
ridge drops slightly then rises again; in places it is extremely narrow
and care must be taken, though a rope is not essential. The view into
the cirque is impressive. Reach the Pène Blanque (2905m). E of this
summit the cirque wall is split by a deep cleft, the Clé de Curé. To
avoid this drop to the S of the ridge, obliquely on scree and boulders;
cross the southern slopes beneath the cleft then climb back diagonally
to the ridge. Follow it to Mont Arrouy (2888m) and to the Col de la
Munia. From here, as for the Munia described above. $4\frac{1}{2}$-5h. from
carpark.

Continuation round the eastern curve of the ridge is rather more complicated; before starting on it remember that there is no easy exit from
the ridge until the Col de la Sède at its NE end is reached. From the
Pic de Troumouse, N to the Pic de Gerbats, the ridge forms the top
of the very steep 500m Barroude wall, a preserve of rock climbers and
reached from the upper Aure valley (qv).

From the Munia summit go down the ridge NE and turn a gully-head
by dropping to the R(E) of the crest. Regain the ridge, cross a second
gully-head and continue along the crest to the next main top, Serre-
Mourène (3090m). From this point descend steeply to a saddle; rope
advisable. Follow the ridge to the Pic de Troumouse (3085m).

The ridge now runs due N; follow it without difficulty to pt.3028; it narrows here and care should be taken. Drop down to a saddle, keeping to the L, then climb to the sharp ridge leading to the Pic Heid (3022m). Continue to the Petit Pic Blanc (2957m) and, on boulders, come down to another saddle before climbing by a series of terraces to pt. 2895. Onwards with no difficulty until you approach the Pic de Gerbats, a curious rock tower astride the ridge. This is turned on its L(W) side, passing nearly 200m below the Gerbats summit (2904m). Ignore a ledge line under the tower proper; well below this descend diagonally L on shifting scree (cairns) and climb a short slab. Cross a rib and go down on the other side to a ledge; follow ledge to a little saddle on a spur of the Gerbats. Ascend a gully to rejoin the ridge now heading NW some distance from the Gerbats. So follow crest NW without further difficulty to the Col de la Sède (2651m), $3\frac{1}{2}$-4h. from Pic de la Munia.

From the col descend SW into the cirque over rock and grass slopes, then continue W down the lower slopes to reach a path coming up from Héas, above the true R bank of the Gave des Touyères, and near the Aires cabin. Turn R down this path which leads to the Héas chapel. Alternatively, for those wishing to return to the carpark, a path below the Aires cabin contours S and W in a huge semi-circle for 3km at 2050/2100m to a hut at pt. 2099, where a short track SW runs almost horizontally to the roadhead. $1\frac{1}{2}$-2h. from Col de la Sède, 5-6h. from the Munia, minimum for round trip 11h. without significant halts.

ROBIÑERA	3003m	2989m IGC
CHINIPRO	2800m	2784m IGC

These 2 prominent summits in Spain face the S side wall of the Munia group, across the head of a valley called the Circo de La Munia. This mounts at length from the Pineta roadhead to 2 lakes at 2530m below the W side of Robiñera. Seen from the Pic de la Munia, the latter resembles a gigantic slag tip. Nowadays the easiest approach to both tops starts from a motorable forestry road running WNW from Parzan village (1144m) on the Bielsa tunnel road, up the Rio Real valley. From a point about 7km up this valley at c.2000m a path climbs N on the W side of the Barranco del Clot to the Collado de las Puertas (2525m), just S of the southern Munia lake. So attain the Chinipro easily to the W ($2\frac{3}{4}$h. from road), or the Robiñera to the NE by a broad spur ($3\frac{1}{4}$h. from road).

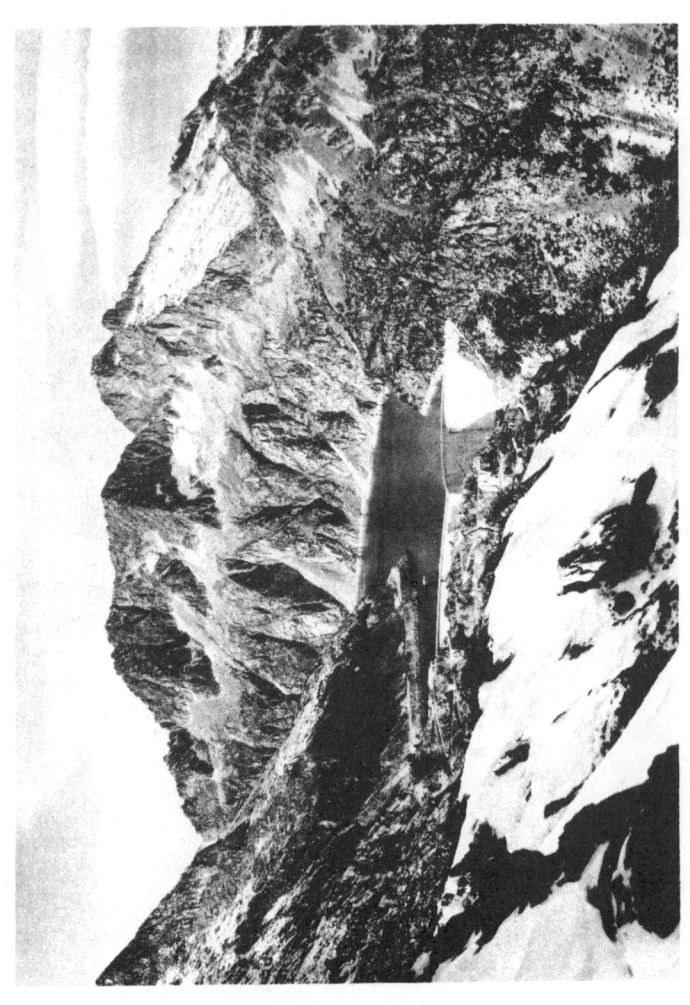

Turon de Néouvielle, Trois Conseillers and Pic de Néouvielle above the Lac de Cap de Long.

Néouvielle group

Maps: IGN 50m. n.1747, 1748. IGN/RP 50m. n.4,5. IGN 25m.V n.275, 276. IGN 25m. DB n.1747W, 1747E, 1748W.

The Néouvielle area is one of high granite peaks, lakes and pines. It lies S of the Barèges - Tourmalet road, N of the Cirque de Troumouse and E of the Gave de Pau valley. It is a large area without villages, and without roads until the electricty board (EDF) built the road from Fabian in the Aure valley to the dam of the Lac de Cap de Long in 1959. All other approaches to the area necessitate long marches.

The principal summits are the Pic Long (3192m), Pic de Néouvielle (3091m), Pic Badet (3160m), Pic de Campbieil (3173m) and Pic Méchant (2944m). The area is particularly suited to camping. The most convenient permanent base is the TCF Chalet-Refuge (1852m) standing above the E end of the Lac Orédon, reached by a short side road from the new one leading up to the Lac d'Aubert. See note in Huts section about this TCF site.

Refuge-Hôtel de la Glère   2120m

Start from Barèges on the Col du Tourmalet road N.618(D.918); the hut is situated 4.5km to the S, as the crow flies; now possible to go by car. A signpost in the village street of Barèges indicates where to start; go along a little road to the upper S side of the village. This soon becomes a track, which rises in zigzags and reaches extensive woods cut by a number of walks and ski tracks. The track to be followed climbs in wide bends and, after passing a ski-jump, comes into the open in the Glère valley at a point where a small motor road now arrives from the N.618, having begun 1.5km E of the village. So follow the road S up the valley beside the stream and finish by zigzags at the Lac de la Glère (2103m). Then the track climbs a little way up to the large hut overlooking the lake (3h. on foot).

Note: The usual way from this hut/inn to the nearest of the major tops, the Pic de Néouvielle, is a walk and scramble of about 5h.

Refuge Packe   2509m

This small hut lies 2.5km W of the Pic de Néouvielle and about 3.5 km SSW of the Glère inn. It is not particularly well situated as a

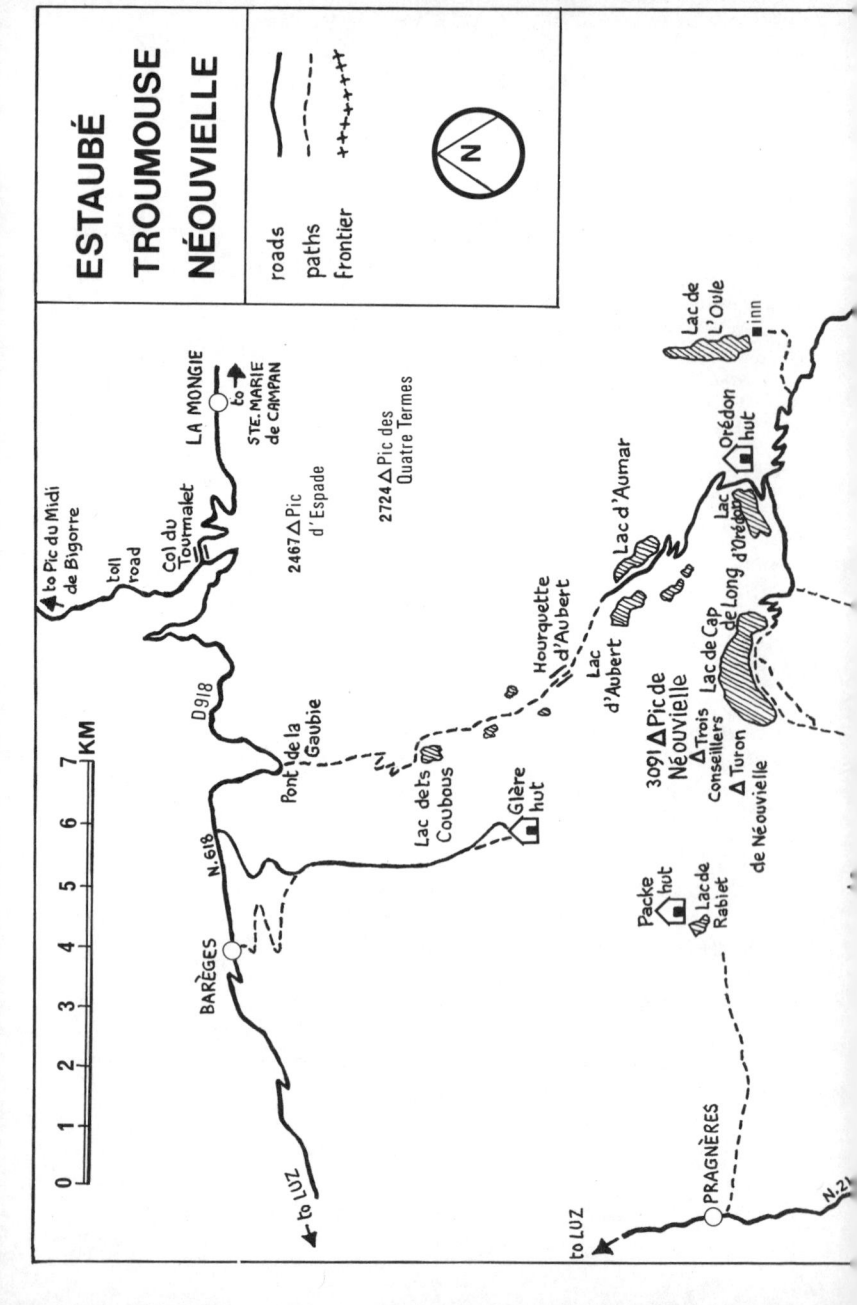

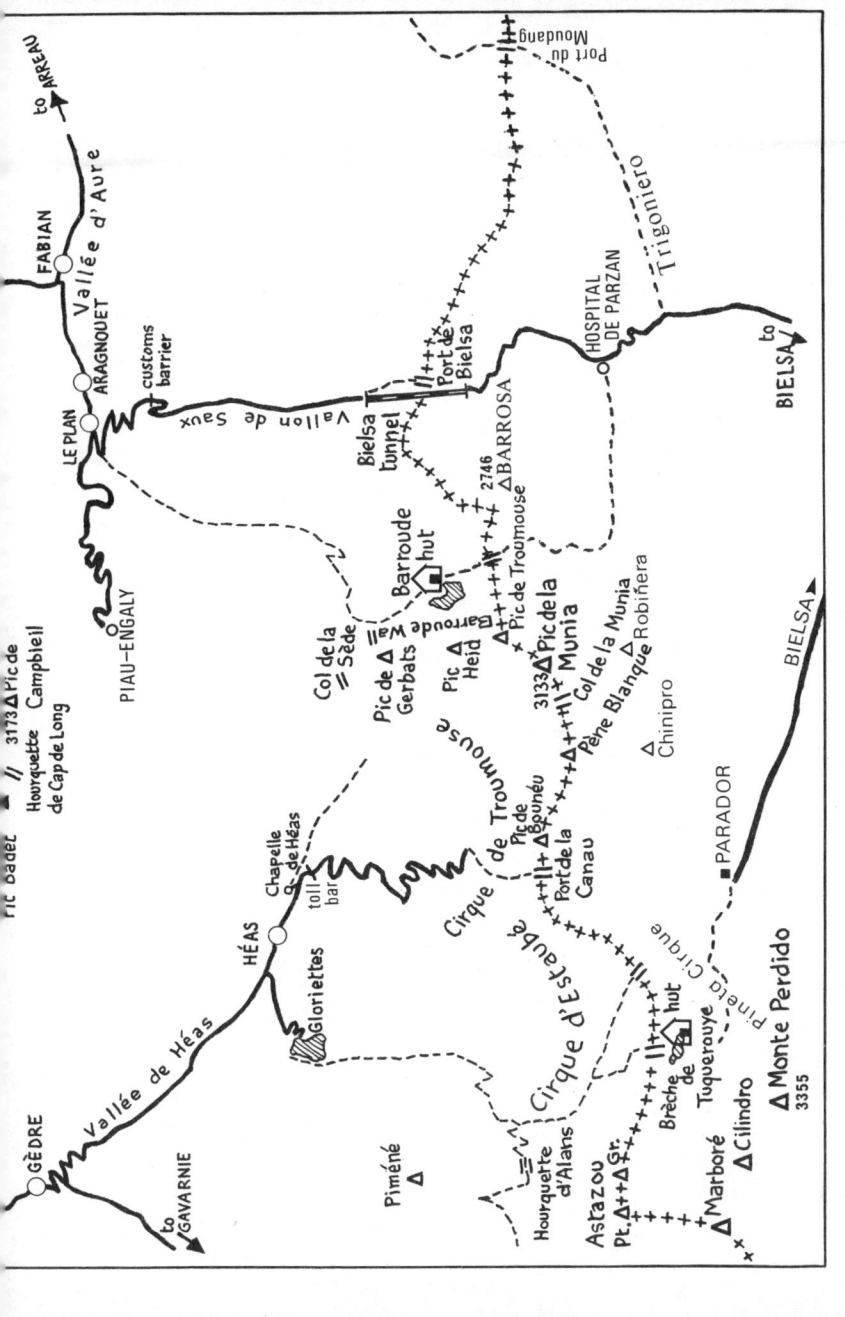

base for any of the major summits. The PNP has improved the path from
the Glère inn up the Pourtet valley by which the hut is best reached in
$1\frac{3}{4}$ h. The long route from Pragnères up the Barrada valley, described in
previous editions of the guide, is not really recommended. There is a
shorter way ($4\frac{1}{2}$ h.) from a new roadhead at the Estibe (1400m), above
and SE of Luz St. Sauveur.

Refuge Campana de Cloutou   2225m

Though somewhat distant from the main Néouvielle summits, this hut is
conveniently placed for quite interesting ascents such as the Pic des
Quatre-Termes (2724m), Pic du Contade (2714m), Pic de Bastan (2721m)
etc. The hut was rebuilt in 1979 and is best reached from the N.618
(D.918) road on the E side of the Tourmalet col between La Mongie and
Ste. Marie de Campan.

At a point 3.5km below La Mongie, where the road makes a sharp hair-
pin bend, take a good path S, clearly signposted (GR 10c). It leads up
first to the Caderolles lake (2041m) and passes along the W shore; then
it ascends a little to the much larger Gréziolles lake, and beyond this
due S to the hut on NE side of the Campana lake (3h. from main road).

Refuge d'Orédon   1852m

From Barèges, over the Hourquette d'Aubert (2498m); recommended
pedestrian approach from the NW. About 4km along the N.618 road
(D.918), just after the Gaubie bridge (1538m) and a small café, follow
bold GR 10 waymarks on a path S for 1.5km. Cross a small tributary
stream, where the path leads W across the valley-side and soon turns S
again, winding up to the Coubous lake (2041m). Cross the dam (E) to
where the track slants above the lake to gain height S, passing large
pools and taking a depression between pleasant lakes to a series of zigzags going up more steeply to the Aubert col ($2\frac{1}{2}$ h.). On the other
side a good path descends ESE towards the ridge of low ground between
the Aubert and Aumar lakes, which now carries the extended road from
the carpark at its S end (45 min., $3\frac{1}{4}$ h. from Gaubie bridge). This road
is due to be completed all the way up to the Aubert col. Continue by
the road for 4.5km to hut-inn beside the Orédon lake; from Aubert
carpark, a better way adopts a track SE, along the N sides of a string
of small lakelets (Laquettes), rejoining the road over halfway down.

Normally, parties reach the hut-inn by car or taxi along the D.929
from Vielle-Aure.

PIC DE NÉOUVIELLE   3091m

Or, Pic d'Aubert. Normal route, F. From the Orédon hut-inn, take road to carpark beside the Aubert lake (2148m). A service track crosses the dam at S end of lake. Now a vaguely marked path mounts and circles SW and NW round a spur, crossing latter at pt.2439 - the foot of Crête de Barris d'Aubert. Round the other (N) side, descend a little at first, then go up W through a large boulderfield, following a line of small cairns and heading directly for the peak. One line of cairns bears R(WNW) and leads to the Br. de Chausenque (2790m), clearly in view; ignore this. Continue over low rock terraces SW on to the snowy Ramoun glacier on NE side of peak and, keeping R of the Ramoun ridge gap (2965m), mount this to its highest point. Leave the glacier following cairns and traces of a path under the NE facet, and climb by easy ledges R to a point on the NNE spur, where a path is met coming up from the N. Bear L and scramble over easy rocks to the summit ($3\frac{1}{2}$ h. from Aubert carpark).

There is a fine view, with a long shattered ridge running S to the Pic Long in the middle distance, and Monte Perdido beyond. To the SW is the line of the Gavarnie peaks; to the W the Vignemale. Prominent to the N is the Pic du Midi de Bigorre with its high TV mast. The view down on to the lakes of Cap de Long and Orédon is impressive.

PIC DE NÉOUVIELLE   NE side

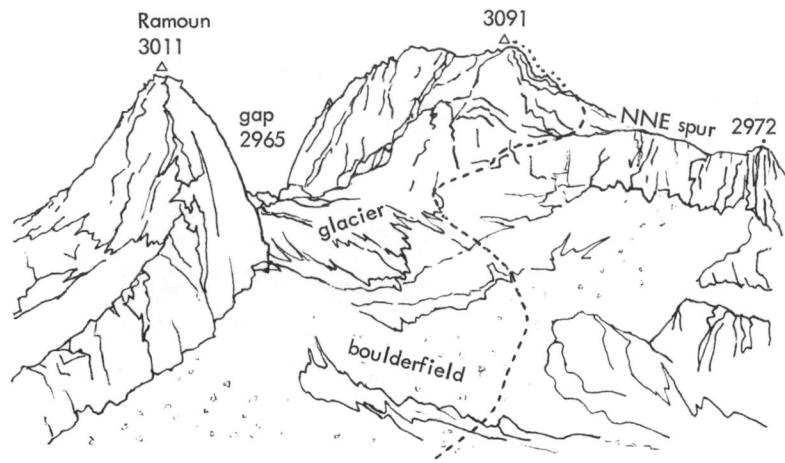

Pic Long N face, with Pic Badet to the rear.

PIC LONG 3192m

Usual route. Grade, F. Start from the roadhead carpark/dam at E end of Cap de Long lake (2161m). The carpark is subject to stonefall. Go down W to lakeside path along S shore (stonefall), where the steep SE side of the Néouvielle, dropping into the lake, is an impressive sight. Due to potential falling rock in rainy weather, the lakeside track is now quitted after one km for a zigzag ascent and a contouring path above the lake, so that one traverses into the broad valley S of the lakehead, called Montagne de Cap de Long; this is reached at a point where streams converge at c.2300m. The massive Pic de Campbieil is seen at the head of this valley.

Ascend on the R(W) side of the stream convergence, going up the valley steeply till above pt.2527, with cairns marking the route over rock terraces and boulders. So approach the foot (2786m) of a long lateral moraine running out E into the valley from the Pic Maubic, a subsidiary of Pic Long. Turn the end of the moraine and go up W to the foot of snow slopes beneath the Pays Baché glacier flowing from Pic Long. A little to the L of the summit cone, note a small notch in the SE ridge, the Hourquette du Pic Long (3099m). Head up the glacier towards this notch, with a steepening finish on snow from which a sometimes awkward entry is made into a chimney above, depending on the height of snow against the rock. Climb the steep chimney which is otherwise not difficult (30m) to the notch. Go up the ridge then follow a ledge L onto the S face, from where a steep but fairly easy gully leads to the top (5h. from carpark).

Pic Long N face technical climbs

The face is about 600m high above Lac Tourrat, and is partly glacier covered. The first route was made in 1933 by Robert Ollivier and Roger Mailly, a team noted for very difficult climbs on the Pic du Midi d'Ossau. Since then other routes have been made, all of considerable difficulty, D to TD. Lac Tourrat can be reached from the W end of Lac de Cap de Long by following a steep, cairned streambed to the col Hourquette de Bugarret (2614m); then descending its W side to the Bugarret tarn infall which leads S over rock terraces, slabs and rough ground to the Lac Tourrat (about 4h. from roadhead). A shorter way lies over the Col Tourrat (2604m) further S, going up the R(S) side of the Bugarret ravine (3h.).

PIC DE CAMPBIEIL 3173m

Position and height omitted on most printings of map n.276. Second in height in the district, standing at the head of the broad valley of the

Montagne de Cap de Long. This large but otherwise undistinguished summit vies with the Taillon above Gavarnie for the dubious reputation of being the easiest 3000m peak in the Pyrenees. Few trouble to walk up it, partly because of its lack of interest and partly because of its distance from the Cap de Long roadhead (Pic Long, above).

For the easiest route, as for Pic Long, keeping up the valley past the Maubic moraine, then a tarn, to the narrow plateau and Hourquette at the top, called the Badet col (2902m). Bear away L(W) to ascend boulders steeply to pt.3157, then NE along the L side of the main ridge to the true top. Extensive view ($5\frac{1}{2}$ h.).

PIC BADET   3160m

A prominent outlier of Pic Long, joined by latter's SE ridge. Easily reached as for Pic Long to the Hourquette du Pic Long (3099m), then by the NW ridge in a scramble of 30 min.

PIC MÉCHANT   2944m

When seen to the S from the Lac de Cap de Long dam, this peak appears as a very sharp cone at the end of a ridge to the E of the obvious Estaragne hollow which opens above the road shortly before it reaches the dam. An easy but tedious ascent. From the road bridge at 2079m follow a path S into the Estaragne hollow. After about 500m leave the path and climb obliquely SE towards the foot (2428m) of a long, steep gully falling from a saddle in the SW ridge between the peak and the Pic des Toudes (2930m). Avoid the gully and climb leaving it a little to the R. On reaching the saddle after a long pull up, follow a track which rises round the S and SE slopes of the summit cone; so come to a gully of boulders on the E side of the cone which leads to the top (3 h. from road).

PIC D'ESPADE   2467m

An attractive rock summit rising immediately S of the Col du Tourmalet.

From La Mongie. Normal route, F. From the village centre at 1723m a path runs W, parallel to the main road to the Tourmalet col, but on the S side of the valley. Follow this path for about 1.5km and, when it turns S and climbs in zigzags up the Coume de Pourteilh below a cable car line, leave it and continue SW on a track towards the Pic d'Espade. The track curves S to the E side of the Pic. This point can be reached in 15min. from the Tourmalet road by a horizontal traverse SSE from the bend at pt.1936 (parking). When due E of the obvious

Col du Pic d'Espade, leave the track and ascend a sea of boulders to the col, N of the main summit. Do not cross the col; ascend steeply on the E slope of the peak to its summit ($2\frac{1}{2}$ h., or $1\frac{3}{4}$ h. from road bend).

PIC DU MIDI DE BIGORRE 2872m

This bulky object standing N of the Col du Tourmalet must have been visited by more people than any other summit in the Pyrenees. Date of first ascent unknown, but regularly ascended by 'bathers' at Bagnères de Bigorre and Barèges before Ramond walked up it in 1787. A timid English lady, Anne Walker, rode to the summit on horseback in 1838 and an observatory almost at the summit was built in 1878. It is now crowned by a television mast and other 'space age' paraphernalia and has suffered the indignity of a motor toll road from the Tourmalet pass to the Laquets inn, with carpark at 2600m. From there an easy path leads to the summit in 45 min. For those unable or unwilling to make this final climb there is a convenient cablecar. The view from the summit is outstanding. The cableway from La Mongie is open to the public only as far as Le Taoulet (2315m); above this station the line is private and serves only the observatory. Numerous technical winter climbs have been made on the mountain in modern times.

L'ARBIZON 2831m

Outlying peak between the Néouvielle district and the Vallée d'Aure. An impressive, isolated rock configuration, especially spurs and pillars on the 600m NW face (several serious climbs), but all sides are precipitous with many rockfaces, except the SW.

Normal (South) Route. Ungraded. From Guchen, about 5km S of Arreau in the Aure valley, branch W on the D.30 road and go past Aulon to the roadhead at Granges de Lurgues (c.1400m). From there follow a path W on the N side of the valley for about 2km. On leaving a copse, turn N and ascend a broad steep valley to just below the Coulariot fountain near pt.2056. Just after this a poor track now mounts N/NE towards a saddle (Br. Ouest, or d'Aurey, 2654m), seen in the undulating ridge between the Arbizon and Monfaucon. Grass terraces give way to schist before the saddle is reached; cairns. Go up the W ridge on boulders to the summit, keeping to the R(S) side; about 5h. from roadhead.

The approach from the N leaves the Ste. Marie de Campan - Col d' Aspin road at Payolle, where a minor road branches S via Pelouse St. Jean to reach the Granges de Camoudiet (1438m, vehicular roadhead). From there somewhat long and complicated routes lead to the Brèche Ouest and to the NW face.

Vallée d'Aure

Maps: IGN 50m. n.1748. IGN/RP 50m. n.4,5. IGN 25m.V n.276.
EA 40m. n.204, 25m. n.205.   IGN 25m. DB n.1748W, 1748E.

This valley runs SW from the attractive little town of Arreau, then W to its head beneath the Pic de Campbieil and the Barroude wall. From Arreau to St. Lary the valley is broad and cultivated; beyond that it becomes a wooded mountain valley, running through Fabian to Aragnouet and the hamlet of Le Plan.

In this district the word for a stream is 'Neste', corresponding with 'Gave' further W. Thus up to Fabian the stream is the Neste d'Aure, to Le Plan it is the Neste d'Aragnouet, and above Le Plan, in the valley curving southwards under the Campbieil slopes, the main stream is the Neste de Badet. Coming down to Le Plan from the SW is the Neste de la Géla.

S of the Aure valley are a number of side valleys penetrating towards the frontier - here comparatively low with minor summits of c.2600m. Separating these parallel valleys are ridges with summits higher than those on the frontier. In general the area between the main valley and the frontier is one for the mountain walker rather than the climber.

Refuge de Barroude   2373m

At Le Plan (bridge, 1337m) the main road continues W to the winter sports centre of Piau-Engaly. Leave this road and take the Bielsa tunnel road D.173 to just round the first bend in this at 1383m. Round the corner, a piste track goes off SW into the Neste de la Géla valley, along the S side of the stream for 3.5km to some huts. Now as a path, here it crosses the stream and commences a long rising traverse on the W side slopes, twisting up to a rain gauge then rising to zigzags over stony slopes and a junction with the traverse path running N-S under the Barroude wall, directly below the E face of the Pic de Gerbats. Go S along the track to reach the hut in one km and slightly above the N end of the Barroude lakes (4h. from Le Plan).

Barroude Wall

Varying in height from 400-500m, this limestone barrier stretches N-S for about 2 km from the Pic de Gerbats to the Pic de Troumouse. Since 1955 several routes of considerable difficulty have been worked out on the wall, notably by the brothers Jean and Pierre Ravier. One of the hardest is a direct line to pt.3028 between the Heid and Troumouse tops (500m, ED-); the Raviers took 9h. to complete the climb in 1962. The NE spur of pt.2957 is a little easier and on better rock, but has a pitch of VI.

FRONTIER AREA

There are no peaks of consequence between the Pic de Troumouse in the W and the Pic de Batoua in the E, a distance of 25km. The wooded valleys leading up to the pastures below the frontier and to the frontier passes are very beautiful and ideal for walking and camping.

Vallon de Saux - Port de Bielsa   2429m

The first valley E of the Neste de la Géla (Barroude hut). From Le Plan it leads up to the Port de Bielsa and now contains the road going to the Bielsa tunnel. The D.173 road has all but obliterated the old path to the col, but from the tunnel entrance (1824m, parking place), 2km from the frontier, the old path exists and can be followed to the Bielsa pass. On the Sp. side the path descends in zigzags, indirectly at first, to the S end of the tunnel, about 6km all told.

Vallée du Moudang

Again, a few km E of the Saux, this longer parallel valley starts opposite the Moudang bridge (1053m, parking and campsite) in the Aure valley, about 1.5km E of Fabian. A broad track follows the W side of the Moudang stream through fine woods for 3km to emerge at pastures, where it continues for 2.5km to the Granges du Moudang group of huts (1521m) in a fork between 2 streams. The spur dividing them is crowned by the Pic de la Hount.

The approach to the Port du Moudang (Sp. Puerto de Trigoniero, and other spellings, 2495m) lies up the stream heading at first SSE, called the Chourrious (the other, SW, is Héchempy). In 1.5km the Chourrious path turns R and soon ascends S across the E slopes of the Pic de la Hount, traversing and ascending obliquely with a move L to the col. On the Sp. side a good path goes down into the Trigoniero valley, past a small hut (1970m); it curves W in a long stretch of forest to join the Bielsa tunnel road at the Sp. customs post (1290m) at a point about 4 km above the Parzan hamlet (1144m, various services). From Granges du Moudang, about 5h.

Vallée de Rioumajou

A major valley, lying E of and again parallel to the others; prominent between the Moudang and Rioumajou valleys is the Pic d'Aret (2939m). About 4km SW of St Lary, a branch road swings back L and enters Tramezaigues hamlet at the valley entrance (963m). It is possible to go to the valley head, 11km distant, by car. The valley is heavily wooded and exceptionally beautiful. The narrow road is good for 3-4km, then it becomes bad and careful driving is required to avoid underside damage. The surface improves again as far as a collection of huts at Frédancon (1394m). From here the road is very bad for 2.5km, then improves a little where it emerges from woods into pasture and so reaches the end at the Hospice de Rioumajou (1560m).

This ancient edifice, the last example of Pyrenean inns of the past, is no longer tenanted, but can be used as a shelter in emergencies. It is used by shepherds. The roadhead commands access to a semi-circle of peaks and passes, from the Pic d'Arriouère (2866m) in the W to the Pic de Batoua (3034m) in the E. The main passes are the Port d'Ourdissétou (2403m), described in the next section of the guide; Port de Plan (2527m) and Port de Cauarère/Madère (2526/2540m) - described below.

Port de Cauarère or Madère   2526/2540m

Various spellings of both names. Most Fr. mapping places the Madère col too far S, at saddle 2602. It is really at the unmarked col between pt.2659 (Pène de Millarioux) and pt.2581; this may be calculated as 2560m. However, the recommended HRP crossing pt. is N again of pt. 2581, at 2526 - the true Cauarère; you go over the frontier slightly above and S of the lowest pt., eg. 2540. This latter crossing pt. is the one described below. Therefore, IGN 25m.V map is incorrect, but the RP one is approximately on the right course.

A short way beyond the Rioumajou hospice the trail divides; go L(ESE) into woods, over the stream, to pick up red waymarks all the way. Go up to what appears to be the back of a moraine and take it following small cairns to a wood; so ascend parallel with the Cauarère ravine to emerge in the open near confluence with the Millarioux stream. Here the track climbs R(SW) towards the Port de Plan; leave the track and descend to cross the latter stream. Now go up steepening ground, often with no path visible, between the 2 streams, on scree and slippery black schist; cairns and red paint splashes. Continue thus directly to col in about 3h. from hospice. Magnificent view of the Posets massif and of the huge whaleback of the Bachimale to the E.

PIC DE BATOUA   3034m

Or Pic de Culfrèda. From the Cauarère col (above), F. Follow the frontier ridge N, mostly on schist with traces of a path to the Pic de

Cauarère (2901m). Continue by the ridge, now NE, over boulders and slabs, keeping to the L(NW) side of crest for one km to the summit in 1¾h. from col, 4¾h. from Rioumajou hospice.

Note: the new map IGN 25m. DB n.1748E has corrected the position of the Port de Cauarère and rectified neighbouring detail entirely in accordance with the propositions described on the previous page.

Barrosa - Ordiceto - Suelza

Maps: IGN 50m. n.1748. IGN/RP 50m. n.4. IGN 25m. V n.276.
EA 40m. n.204, 25m. n.205. IGN 25m. DB n.1748W, 1748E.

Immediately S of the frontier, from the Pic de Troumouse in the W to the Rioumajou headslopes in the E, lies a comparatively little known area now quite accessible thanks to the Bielsa tunnel road. In the W are 3 frontier crossing passes: Port de Barroude, or Barrosa (2534m); Port Vieux (2378m); Port de Bielsa (2429m); the latter is described in the Vallée d'Aure section. In the E of this district is the Port d'Ourdissétou, or Ordiceto (2403m), giving access from the Rioumajou site to the Punta Suelza and Punta Fulsa, as well as to the high Ordiceto lake.

Lago Ordiceto 2369m

From Barroude hut by the Port de Barroude (2534m)

The construction of the fine highway S from the Bielsa tunnel makes this pedestrian approach somewhat tedious. From the Barroude hut (2373m) follow the path S and climb to the Port de Barroude, 1.5km from hut. Before descending into the Barrosa cwm, a recommended diversion can be made to the Pico de Barrosa (2746m), standing a little S of the frontier; go E along the frontier crest, a little below it on the Sp. side with traces of a path here and there; in one km reach the Soum de Barroude (2674m), then go SE along a narrow ridge for about 500m to the Pico. Pleasing viewpoint.

Leaving the Port de Barroude, the path descends roughly and with slippery bits into the Circo de Barrosa. It is not always distinct in the upper part. First it leads S, then W to zigzag down rocky terraces. Further down, grass is reached before the path drops to the valley bed. Ford the stream and continue E down the valley for 3km, to where the path reaches the Bielsa tunnel road at the Hospital de Parzan (bunkhouse here). Continue down the main road for 2km to the Sp. customs post, and for a further 2km to the point where an Electricity Board road branches E, signposted to the Lago Ordiceto, 11km. Follow this road, which is driveable, to the Ordiceto power station in 6km. From here the road climbs, curving SE to the Paso de los Caballos (2320m), then proceeds a little higher SW to the lake.

Suelza (L) and Fulsa (R), overlooking the Ordiceto lake, seen from the N.

On the W bank stands the former Ordiceto hut, now abandoned though useable in an emergency. Camping is recommended. If walked all the way, with no lifts on roads, 7-8 h.

From Hospice de Rioumajou by the Port de Ourdissétou (2403m)

Though the lake can be reached by car from the Bielsa tunnel road (see above), those without transport may find it more satisfying to walk there after camping at the hospice. Set off from the Rioumajou site (1560m) following the path S. At the first fork take the R-hand branch, which climbs alongside woods then, in zigzags, rises on to pastures. From here pass through woods again and climb steadily to the frontier at the Ourdissétou saddle. On the Sp. side drop down obliquely S across slopes of the valley to join the road a short distance below the Paso de los Caballos. Then, briefly, as for the previous route (3h. from Rioumajou).

PUNTA SUELZA 2973m

NW ridge normal route. Grade, F+. From the old hut on the W bank of the Ordiceto lake follow traces of a path S, making for the obvious gap of the Collada Suelza (2620m), the lowest point on the skyline of the ridge joining the Suelza (L) and the Fulsa (R). Reach this gap by climbing on good rock. Now go up the NW ridge, keeping a little below the crest on S side, to arrive at the summit after clambering up a short and fairly easy chimney. Extensive panorama all round (2 h.).

PUNTA FULSA 2858m

Normal Route. Grade, PD. Start as for the Suelza (above) and before reaching the Collada find a cairned track to the R, traversing the slope beneath the Suelza-Fulsa ridge, a little below the 2600m contour. Pass under the Fulsa NE face and climb boulders to an obvious col just N of the summit cone. From here climb the N ridge and keep slightly below crest on E side. Scramble up a chimney obstructed by a jammed block; turn this without much difficulty and follow ledge L to attain the summit (3h.).

Trigoniero Valley

Further N than the one ascended for the Ordiceto lake, and described (in descent) in the Moudang part of the Vallée d'Aure section, this long valley gives access from the Bielsa tunnel road at the Sp. customs post to the rarely visited summits of Arriouère (Ibonet, 2866m) and the Pic de l'Espade (Ordiceto, 2832m); both are more easily approached from the Rioumajou hospice in France.

Southern Limestone Range

Map: EA 25m. n.231 Cotiella zone.

The eastern end of this range lies far to the S of the frontier, at the limit of the Pyrenees. The Cotiella massif is the highest point of the whole sub-range, which stretches from the Bisaurin in the Western Pyrenees. SW of the Cotiella is the Peña Montañesa, and to the SE the Turbón, almost 30 km S of the frontier; the EA map for the latter has not yet been published (1987).

COTIELLA MASSIF

A mountain of huge proportions, outstripping any comparable summit-massif in the Pyrenees. Moreover, the Cotiella lies hidden from any road, although it is seen in the distance from Monte Perdido, Posets, and the Maladeta massif. Much frequented by local hill walkers while foreigners are rarely seen; tremendous panorama.

It lies S of Plan, in the Cinqueta valley, and W of the Ésera valley. The massif consists of an undulating ridge curving round the large Circo de Armeña on its E side; the summit rises towards the S of the curve and the Pico d'Espouy and Las Coronas somewhat to the N. The Armeña hut stands within the cirque, which higher up is riddled with scores of caves and pots; these are also numerous on the W/NW side of the massif.

This region was visited by Henry Russell in 1865, when he was disturbed by wolves while sleeping in his sheepskin sack in the cirque, and again in 1870, when he slept on the summit of Cotiella and was attacked by bandits during his night journey back to Plan. Neither wolves nor bandits are likely to be met nowadays.

Refugio de Armeña 1860m

Reach the village of Barbaruens (1128m) from the Ésera valley by road of 8 km, leading NW from the village of Seira, 20 km SW of Benasque. Now follow a forest track NW, rising steeply over slabs. After some 30 min. the path bears W and climbs above the Bilsé stream; there follows a steep ascent through woods to reach the Collado del Ibón (1900m). From here descend a little to the Armeña tarn (1846m) among pines. Continue NNW over level ground for one km. to the hut ($3\frac{1}{2}$ h.).

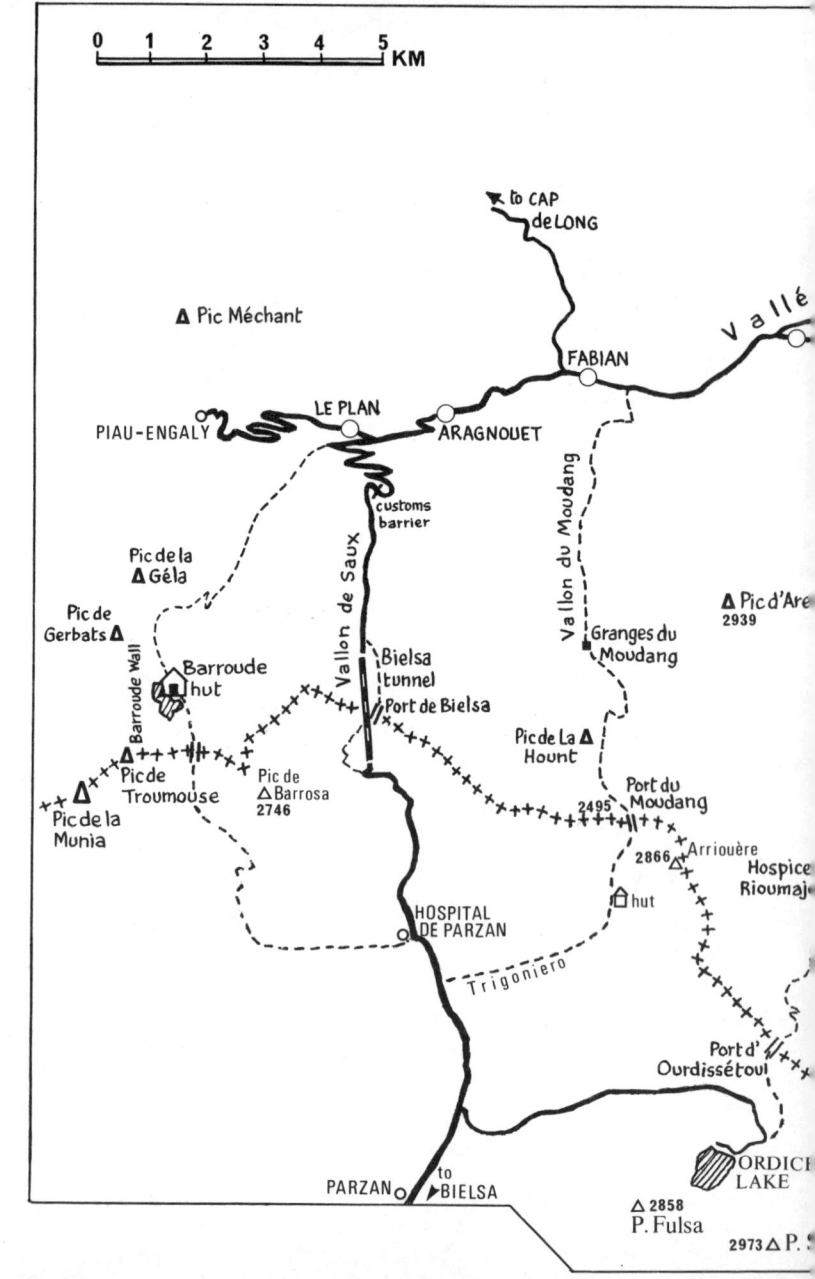

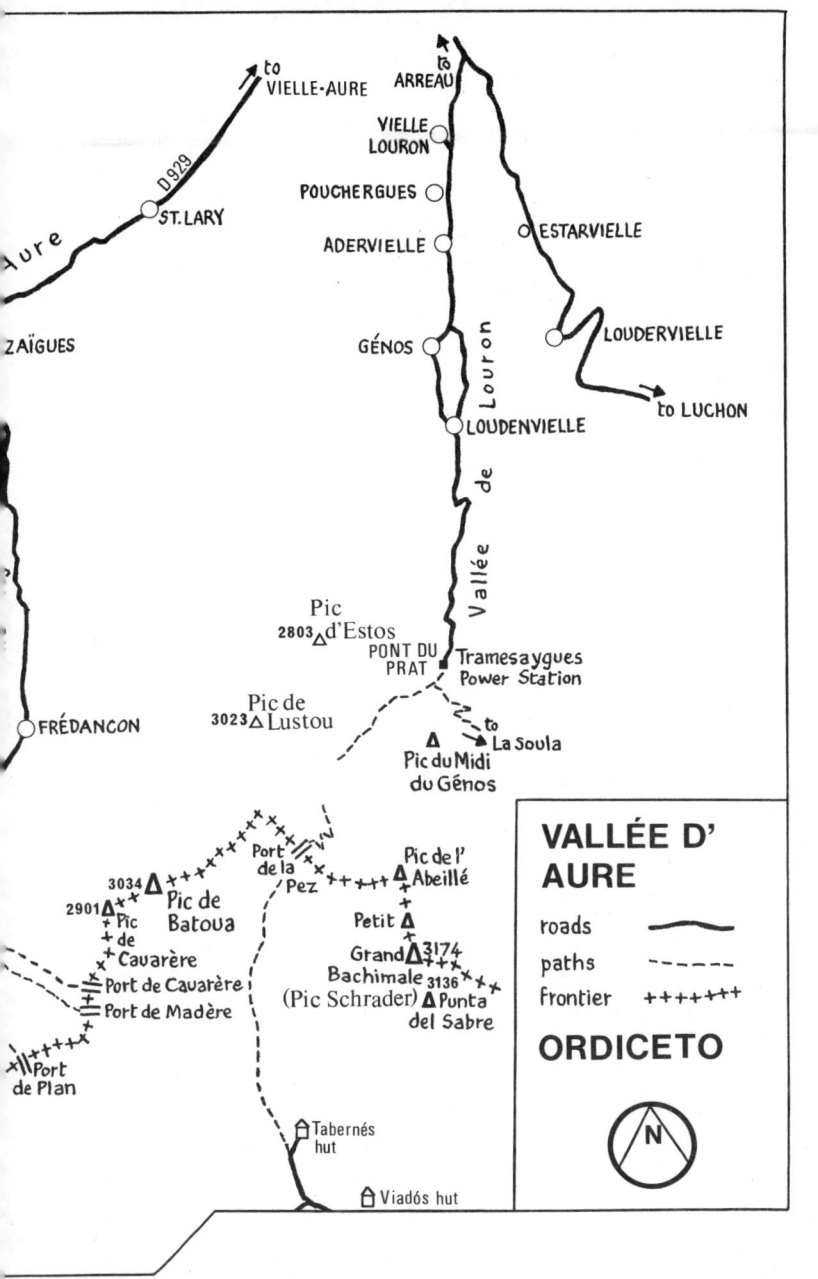

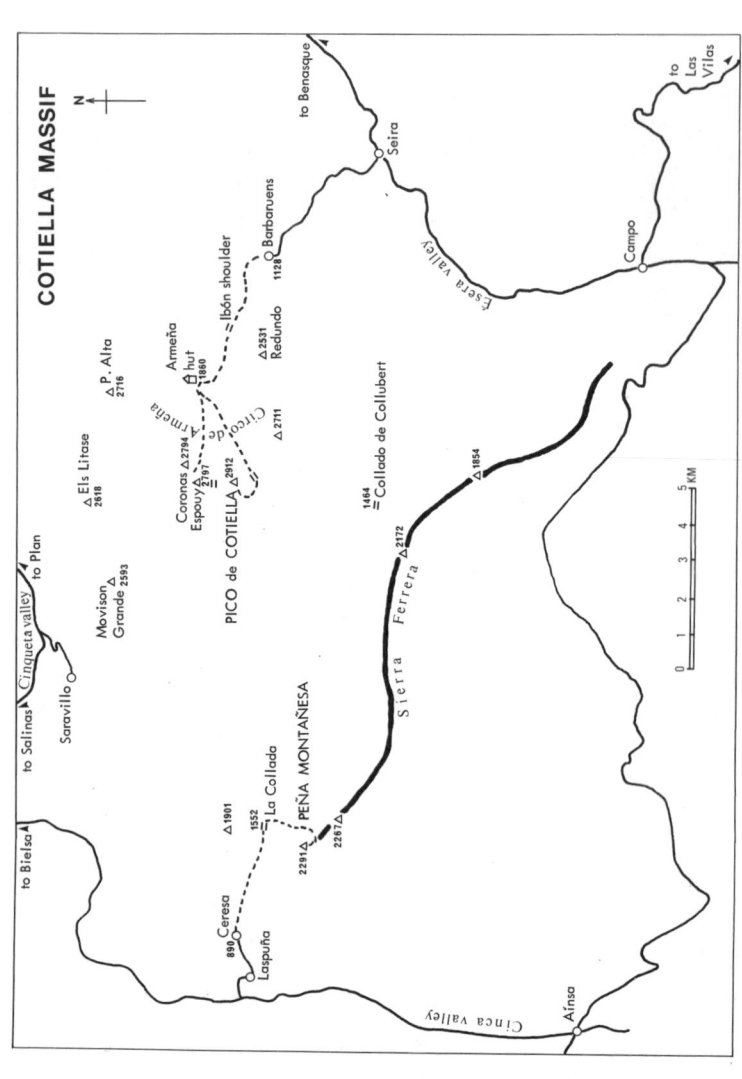

PICO DE COTIELLA 2912m

Normal Route. Grade, F. From the Armeña hut start on a line SW over grass and boulders, towards the summit. After 500m bear S then again SW and climb steadily towards the Collado de Cotiella, a saddle SE of the summit. Go up steeply on boulders to this saddle at c.2660m. Follow L side of ridge and contour round to W side of the summit; ascend an easy chimney to the top ($3\frac{1}{2}$-4h.).

PICO DE ESPOUY 2797m

Normal Route. Ungraded. As for the Cotiella route (above) for about one km. Then bear R towards the gap between the Espouy and Las Coronas, to its N. Climb steeply on boulders to this gap. From here follow crest to the summit. Though without difficulty, the climb to the col is laborious ($3\frac{1}{2}$h.).

LAS CORONAS 2794m

Grade, AD. As for the Espouy route (above) to the main ridge gap, Brecha Espouy-Coronas (2777m). Here turn to an almost vertical reddish rockface and climb it on poor limestone. At the top of the face go along the crest ENE towards the summit; cross a gap on loose rock by keeping to the L(N) side of the crest. After this the narrow crest leads to the summit (4-5h.).

Note: the horseshoe traverse of the Cotiella ridge is an ambitious exercise (AD), normally done N to S, starting at the Punta Alta (2716) directly above the Armeña hut and finishing properly at the Redundo (2531), where a cavers' track descends to the hut; a shorter finish is to descend the normal route from the Collado de Cotiella. Time for round trip, 12-14h.

PEÑA MONTAÑESA 2291m

A great promontory marking the highest point of the Sierra Ferrera, 20 km in length and forming part of the main southern limestone range. It lies between the lower Cinca and the lower Ésera valleys, and NE of the small town of Ainsa (519m). This culminating point is at its NW end, situated 5km ESE of Laspuña village (709m) in the Cinca valley.

Though of modest height, the southern wall of this sierra is impressive, girt with big cliffs and standing above a relatively low countryside. Laspuña lies just outside the EA map area but the roadhead at Ceresa is at the edge of the map.
The Sierra Ferrera is divided from the Cotiella massif proper by the broad Collubert saddle (1464m), which is crossed by a tractor road.

Normal Route. Ungraded. From Laspuña a road leads to Ceresa hamlet (890m) in 2.5km. Either take a path from top of the hamlet, behind the church, heading ESE up to La Collada (1552m); or from the outskirts of the hamlet a forestry piste road winds up at length to the same saddle - only recommended to car drivers. A small path ascends our peak on the L side of its N ridge; go up to a long steep sweep of boulders. Climb this section keeping to the L, then take a big gully, Canal Ancha, to a saddle on the main SE ridge (2144m). Follow this to top (4-5h. from Laspuña).

Note on rock climbs: there is considerable scope for new routes of up to 450m on the N, W and S walls of the Montañesa and on the long Sierra Ferrera.

EL TURBÓN   2492m

See note about mapping at head of this section. The most southerly point of the southern limestone range; it lies S of the Castejón de Sos to Vilaller road running between the Ésera and Noguera Ribagorzana valleys. There is no hut in the vicinity.

The mountain can be approached from the S by a 16km road that forks E from the Ésera valley at Campo village and leads to the Balneario de las Vilas, 3km S of the summit. It can be reached also from the N by a 3km road that branches S from the Castejón de Sos - Vilaller road, 9km from Castejón, to the hamlet of San Feliú.

Departing from Las Vilas Baths, follow a track N, on the L side of a stream and climb to a saddle on the E ridge. Now ascend along the curving ridge, first on its S side then on its N, to the top (3-4h.).

Coming from San Feliú (1415m) follow a track S as far as the hamlet of La Muria. Drop down to cross a stream, then follow a path leading SW to the Puerto de la Muria (1550m). At this saddle leave the path, which descends to Campo, and climb E to a knoll planted with pines and to a small saddle. Having crossed this, turn R on the NE side of the ridge. Re-cross the ridge and descend slightly onto grass and continue along a path that mounts towards the S, heading into moraine and boulders. Ascend this ground to a pass on the curving E ridge which is followed to the top (5-6h.).

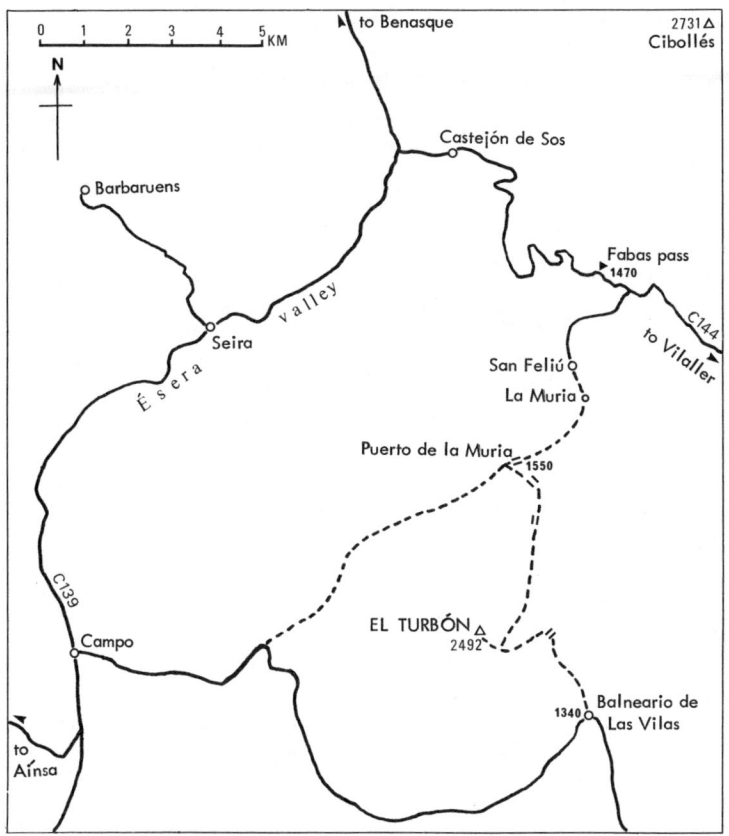

Frontier · I

PORT DE LA PEZ TO THE PIC DES CRABIOULES

Maps: IGN 50m. n.1848. IGN/RP 50m. n.5. EA 25m. n.205, 206.

The distance along this section of the frontier is about 25km. It is the highest continuous stretch of frontier in the whole range and is marked by several interesting summits of over 3000m. 2 high parallel ridges branch NW from the Gourgs Blancs and a third high ridge runs N from the Crabioules. These have summits of equal interest. The southern slopes of this frontier section rise as a great rampart above the upper Estós valley, and S of this lies the great Poset massif.

This area is reached from the N by 2 main routes: the Louron valley running S from Arreau, and the Vallée d'Oô leading up from the road between the Col de Peyresourde and Luchon.

Port de la Pez   2451m
Refugio de Viadós   1760m IGN

Military mapping puts the Viadós hut at 1810, IGC at 1740. From the head of the Louron valley, the shortest way to reach this hut is a long hike over the Pez col. The hut is an important base for touring and climbs in the Posets massif. The Louron valley road ends at Pont de Prat and the Tramesaygues power station (1240m), 7km S of the last village (Loudenvielle, camping, etc.); layby for parking. The sharp peak of the Pic du Midi de Génos rises above the power station, dividing the valleys of the Clarabide (E) and the Pez (W).

Take the path through the power station compound and turn R outside its southern perimeter fence. The path turns half L into woods, with the Pez stream below to R. At a fork (1345m) keep R and continue above the stream to a footbridge (1375m). Cross to the R side and ascend in woods steeply for a short way. Emerging from them, the path is lost in flat open pastures of the broad Pez valley; shepherds' hut on your R, and the Pez col is seen ahead. Vague tracks proceed over pasture to the stream bank; go up the R side to the foot of the buttress where a tributary runs from under a snow patch. Cross the snow and continue to rise, somewhat above the main stream, and cross a torrent coming down from the R.

Slopes beneath the col are steep and have some snow. Above, on the W slope of the valley, the entrance to a tunnel can be seen. This is a relic of a project started in 1771 to put a tunnel under the frontier to facilitate the export of lumber to Spain. Water trouble caused the work to be abandoned before much of the tunnel had been dug. One can only be astonished by the unlikely site chosen for this enterprise. Go up the slopes towards the col, bearing L to where traces of a zigzag path are picked up ($3-3\frac{1}{2}$h. from roadhead). To the SW is the Pic de Batoua; to the SE the Bachimale, with its S ridge running down into Spain.

On the Sp. side bear R then L and drop steeply down the R side of the stream, the Cinqueta de la Pez. Follow this bank for 5km until a hut is reached, the Culrueba (1800m). Carry on down this side to a forestry piste road crossing the stream at the Tabernés bridge (it goes up briefly to end at the Tabernés forestry hut, 1700m). A few zigzags in the piste, still on R side of stream, come down to the Camallón bridge (1670m). Cross here and follow road curving L, passing the junction (1605m) going down the main Cinqueta valley, to make a gradual ascent E to the Viadós hut above buildings beside the Orieles stream ($3\frac{1}{2}$-4h. from Port de la Pez).

Refuge de la Soula   1700m

From head of Louron valley (as for Port de la Pez route above), just to the fork in woods at 1345m. Go L and follow good mule path in beech woods on the N slopes of the Midi de Génos. The path comes into the open above the deep Gorges de Clarabide (1h.). It passes along ledge high above the ravine for one km, then falls and crosses the stream by a bridge to the E side (sometimes washed away). Follow the edge of a little plain to the Soula power station. The hut is in an administrative building to the L; entrance at E end ($1\frac{1}{2}$h. from roadhead).

This site lies at the foot of the Pic de Quartau which divides the valley. The Clarabide valley to the SE rises to the Lac de Pouchergues and the Port de Clarabide. To the E the valley leads up to the Lac de Caillauas and the high valley of the Gourgs Blancs.

GRAND BACHIMALE   3174m   3177m IGC

Universally, Pic Schrader. Sp. Pico de Bachimala (Machimala). The summit is situated at the apex of a Y ridge promontory, detached SW entirely into Spain and 300m distance from the frontier ridge corner apex, inverted 180° to the summit Y ridge, and called Pte. Ledormeur (3120m). Named in honour of Franz Schrader the Pyrenean cartographer who made the first ascent. In fact, the highest point on a long N to S ridge that lies to the E of the Cinqueta de la Pez valley. Several summits occur on this ridge, none of them very pronounced: Pic de l'Abeillé (3029m), Petit Bachimale (3061m), Grand Bachimale (3174m)

and the Punta del Sabre (3136m). At the summit ridge junction called
Ledormeur the frontier turns ESE along the watershed ridge.

Normal Route. Grade, PD. From the Soula hut drop down behind
the power station, cross a footbridge and follow a path that curves round
under the Pic de Quartau into the Clarabide valley, rising to the SE.
Continue along the flank of the Quartau ridge, gradually approaching
the stream. Before reaching it, the path climbs more steeply but bearing away from it; it then drops slightly and meets the stream at a point
where another stream coming from the valley of Aygues-Tortes joins it
at pt. 1937.

Cross the main Clarabide stream and follow the L side of the Aygues-
Tortes stream to a shepherds' hut. Continue W up the valley as far as
pt. 2279. The long line of the Bachimale ridge is seen ahead. Now go
NW and climb a long and rather tedious spur of schist, rising to a point
on the ridge midway between the Pic de l'Abeillé and Petit Bachimale.
Follow the crest S without difficulty, though narrow in places, along
to the junction at Pte. Ledormeur. Scramble down S into a gap and exit
by a steep slope of boulders to a vertical wall under the summit. Turn
this on the R and go up to the top (6-7h. from La Soula). Fine view
of the Posets and the long line of frontier peaks to the E.

Sp. side routes. From the Viadós hut, the usual way goes up the long
S ridge to the Collado de Señal de Viadós (2528m), where it becomes
steeper and more serious. A track makes a rising traverse N over the
slopes far below ridge on its W side; it then goes up the L side of the
SW spur, eventually finishing along the shattered, short W ridge, F+
(5h.). Finishing up the S ridge direct, over the Punta del Sabre, PD.
Another route goes NE up the long Cinqueta de Añes Cruces valley,
nearly to the tarn (2669m) under the Upper Aygues-Tortes (or Cruces)
col (2683m) on the frontier. On the L is the prominent E spur of the
Punta del Sabre. This is climbed (AD) to finish along the S ridge.

Soula hut to Estós hut by the Port de Clarabide

As for the Grand Bachimale (above), to shepherds' hut on L side of the
Aygues-Tortes stream. A little beyond the hut, turn L on a path leading up to the Lac de Pouchergues. Pass round the SW side of the lake,
then bear R and climb more steeply over boulders beneath the pointed
peak of the Fourche de Clarabide. The Port de Clarabide lies just to
the W(R) of this summit. Bear L(S) and climb the slopes to col (2615m)
and frontier; about 4h. Below and to the S lies the upper Estós valley,
falling eastwards from the Puerto de Gistaín and lying parallel to the
frontier. From the Estós valley a side valley rises to the S: the broad
Valle de la Paul, leading to the Posets.

Descend into a side valley formed by the S ridge of the Fourche de
Clarabide, known as the Fitas de la Coma, and a shorter ridge on its
W side. Head due S until you reach a tiny tarn. Follow R bank of the
stream flowing from it and cross this stream where it is joined by another coming from the NW. Keep to the L bank of the stream, dropping
down by rock terraces, and follow a path until it joins the main path in
the Estós valley. Turn L on this path and follow it along L bank of the
river for a little over 2km. The Estós hut (1835m) will be seen on a
bluff nearby (2h., 6h. from La Soula). The Sp. approaches to the hut
are described in the Posets section of the guide.

PIC DES GOURGS BLANCS 3129m

North Ridge. Grade, PD+. From the Soula hut follow the path
that climbs NE then bears E above a long, shallow gorge below the N
slopes of the Pic de Quartau. Reach a flat area of pasture and a saddle,
from which the Lac de Caillauas is seen below. Beyond the lake a long
valley rises to the SE. To the L of it is the ridge stretching from the
Pic de Hourgade to the Pic des Spijoles. To the R is a lesser ridge, approaching the frontier obliquely and joining it at the Pic des Gourgs Blancs.
Between this summit and the Pic des Spijoles, at the head of the valley,
stands the Pic Gourdon.

Drop down to the dam at the W end of the Lac de Caillauas, near the
Caillauas hut, and cross the dam. Follow a path above the S side of
the lake. Beyond the lake follow the R side of a stream running into it
and walk up through a miniature valley (snow). Cross the stream by a
snowbridge or boulders and bear slightly L. Reach a point above the
Lac des Isclots. Work round its N side and cross a stream flowing into
it from the Lac du Milieu. Continue SE from the lake (traces of path)
and pass between the Lac du Milieu and a small frozen tarn (2523m)
further S. These lakes and a number of small tarns are the Gourgs
Blancs, or White Tarns; they are usually frozen or half frozen.

From pt. 2523 come down slightly then begin a long gentle rise, first
over scree, then snow, on a general line towards the Col des Gourgs
Blancs - a snow saddle between the Pic Gourdon and the Pic des
Gourgs Blancs. There will probably be a clear track in snow to the
saddle. About one km from pt. 2523 turn half R from the track to the
saddle and climb the snow covered glacier to the foot of the N ridge,
thrusting out on to the glacier at 2900m.

Climb onto rock at the lowest point of the ridge. There appears to be
no definite route but it is perhaps best first to bear slightly L then to
return to the crest when about halfway up. A number of chimneys look
promising but not all have practicable exits. The scramble is not difficult but care should be taken. Time may be lost in route finding, as

it is not always easy to see far ahead and some obvious routes run out; allow 5h. from La Soula. The view from the summit is very fine, particularly of the Posets massif.

Refuge d'Espingo   1967m

From Castillon in the Larboust valley above Luchon, a road D.76 runs southwards through the village of Oô to the Granges d'Astau, where cars may be left (1139m). From here follow a broad track S (GR 10), and climb through woods to the Lac d'Oô, 1504m (1h.). This spot has been celebrated for some time. Ramond, passing by here in 1787, noted that it was already a 'must' for visitors to the Luchon spa. It is a circular lake lying in a deep hollow with an impressive backdrop of mountains and a fine waterfall. The inn on the other side of the small dam is on the site of an inn that Russell used as a base for excursions to the frontier peaks and Spain.

Follow the path climbing above the E side of the lake and reach a saddle (1967m). A path branches R to the hut, 200m away; about 3h. from the Granges d'Astau.

S of the hut lies the Lac Saussat and a broad valley with the Pic Quayrat and the Pic Lézat to the E, the sharp Tusse de Montarqué in the centre, and the ridge ending in the Pic des Spijoles to the W. Behind the Tusse de Montarqué rise the summits of the Perdiguère and the Seil de la Baque, both on the frontier. A little below the hut is the Espingo lake at the entrance to the Val d'Arrouge, rising to the W.

Refuge du Portillon   2550/2570m

From the Espingo hut join the main path proceeding S, skirt Lac Saussat, then, after crossing the stream by a bridge, follow the paved path and mount the steps to the SE. At the top of this staircase cross at pt. 2508 a shoulder and continue to hut beneath the Portillon dam (1½h.).

Espingo hut to Estós hut by the Port d'Oô (2908m)

This is a classic route, first described by Ramond in 1787 and already well established. From the Espingo hut join the main path S. Skirt Lac Saussat (path paved with flat slabs) and go on to pt. 2099, where the track crosses the stream by a bridge. Just before reaching bridge turn R(W) and climb grass slopes to a path and scramble up an outcrop. Turn L and climb over some boulders and pass under the NE and E faces of the Pic des Spijoles. Continue to rise, following cairns, to a point where the Lac Glacé can be seen in a hollow to the SE. Go down to a small tarn to the NW of this lake and ascend SW from it until you come to the rock terraces above and to the S of Lac Glacé.

Pic Quayrat, Pic Lézat and the Lac du Portillon from track to the Portillon d'Oô.

Bear SE, passing a small half-frozen tarn beneath the NW end of the
Seil de la Baque glacier. From here climb SW to the obvious pass of
the Port d'Oô, itself bare of snow. The route is marked by cairns, 4h.
Ramond noted that the route was already marked by cairns on the Fr.
side in 1787. He added stones to them as he passed.

This col lies between the Pic Jean Arlaud, a sugar-loaf to the W, and
the ridge rising to the Cap du Seil de la Baque to the E. Seil de la
Baque means Cow Glacier; the outline of the glacier, when viewed
from the valley to the N, is supposed to resemble a cow. It does not;
it may have done so once.

From the pass, drop down then bear L beneath it; then R, leaving the
Lago de Gías to the R. Descend in wide curves to the L then R again
and reach a stream coming down from the Lago de Gías. Cross stream
to its R side and join a path that leads down wooded slopes to the Estós
hut (2h., 6h. from Espingo hut).

PICS DES CRABIOULES   E. 3116m   W. 3106m

Normal Route. Grade, PD-. From the Portillon hut climb the
dam by an iron ladder and turn L along it; at its E end a path curves
round a buttress and starts to ascend eastwards up the Vallon Inf. de
Litérole. Go up the valley, which has the serrated ridge joining the
Pic Lézat to the Crabioules to the L and the Pic Rouge to the R. The
path disappears but the route is obvious as far as the snow saddle of
the Col (Inf.) de Litérole (2983m) on the frontier (2h.).

The peak rises NE of the pass. The 2 summits are at the ends of a
very narrow ridge of about 250m. Another short ridge falls away from
the W top down to the col. Follow cairns to the foot of this ridge and
pass beneath the SW flank as far as the second chimney. Climb this
chimney of about 80m, steep but not difficult, on good holds. It leads
to the W top. The ridge walk to the E top is somewhat exposed and
very sharp; the faces on both sides fall away with considerable steepness (45 min. from col, 2¾h. from hut).

The view N into the cirque of the Lis valley is impressive. To the
SW is the huge mass of the Perdiguère; to the SE the distant gleaming
crest of the Maladeta massif.

PIC QUAYRAT   3060m

Marked Gd. Quayrat on IGN maps. Seen from the Espingo hut, the
most prominent feature to the E of the valley. Its W wall, scarred by
a large number of long, steep-falling ridges and gullies, provides one
of the two important rock climbing faces in this area. There are half

Pic des Spijoles E face.

a dozen routes graded TD, all of about 500m. There are also easier ways to the summit, one on the W face itself and another by the Br. de Quayrat, a saddle in the N ridge of the peak separating it from the Petit Quayrat (2847m). This saddle is not marked by name on IGN maps but is at pt.2749. While the N ridge is easy, the way up to this saddle is complicated and not recommended.

Couloir des Avalanches. Grade, PD. This climb in the centre of the W face is of about 500m. The long straight gully owes its discouraging name to snow avalanches which sweep it in the spring. It is clear of snow in the summer. Rope advised.

From the Espingo hut follow the main track S to the top of the paved staircase above the Coume de l'Abesque. Leave the path, traverse L to cross the main stream and ascend to foot of W face in the summit line. The couloir lies between 2 falling ridges and the climbing starts in a kind of small bay in the rockface from which a short chimney rises to the L. Take the chimney and reach the foot of the gully proper. Climb the gully steadily, following the trough; there are no particular difficulties. The head of the gully is a few m from the summit (5-6h.) It is best to descend the same way.

PIC DES SPIJOLES 3065m

A fine rock peak at the SE end of the ridge that forms the NE side of the Gourgs Blancs valley. The E face, standing above the route from Espingo to the Port d'Oô (see above) shares with the W face of the Quayrat the attention of serious rock climbers. There are a large number of routes and variants graded TD or ED but they are shorter than the Quayrat ones, being of not more than 300m. The rock is granite and generally good. There are easier ways of reaching this summit.

Normal Route. Ungraded. From the Espingo hut follow the way to the Port d'Oô (see above), pass under the E face of the Spijoles and continue to the foot of the SE ridge. Leave the path and work L round the foot of this ridge, climbing on grass then boulders. Continue westwards then slant up to the foot of a chimney seen above in the S facet. Climb this chimney and a boulder slope above, bearing a little to the R; so find a track making towards a second easy chimney which leads up to the summit (4h.).

PIC PERDIGUÈRE 3222m

A massive summit, one of the highest points of the whole frontier, and exceeded only by the Vignemale peaks and the Marboré (Pyrenees W guide). The Sp. route from the Estós hut is straightforward but quite long, by the Perdiguero valley and the ESE ridge (5h.).

Normal Route. Ungraded. From the Portillon hut, as for the Crabioules (see above) to a point on the path at the foot of the Vallon Inf. de Litérole, about 45m above the Lac du Portillon (10 min.). A faint path here branches R and follows the curve of the E end of the lake. Follow it and climb diagonally SSW to the Glacier du Portillon, lying beneath the Portillon d'Oô (not to be confused with the Port d' Oô further W). On reaching the glacier turn SE and climb slopes of boulders and snow to a saddle, the Col Sup. de Litérole (3049m) on the frontier between the Pic Royo (3121m) to the N and the Perdiguère to the S. From this pass turn R and follow ridge to summit ($2\frac{1}{2}$h.). The Posets massif is seen to the SW across the Estós valley. To the E is the Maladeta.

New Estós hut

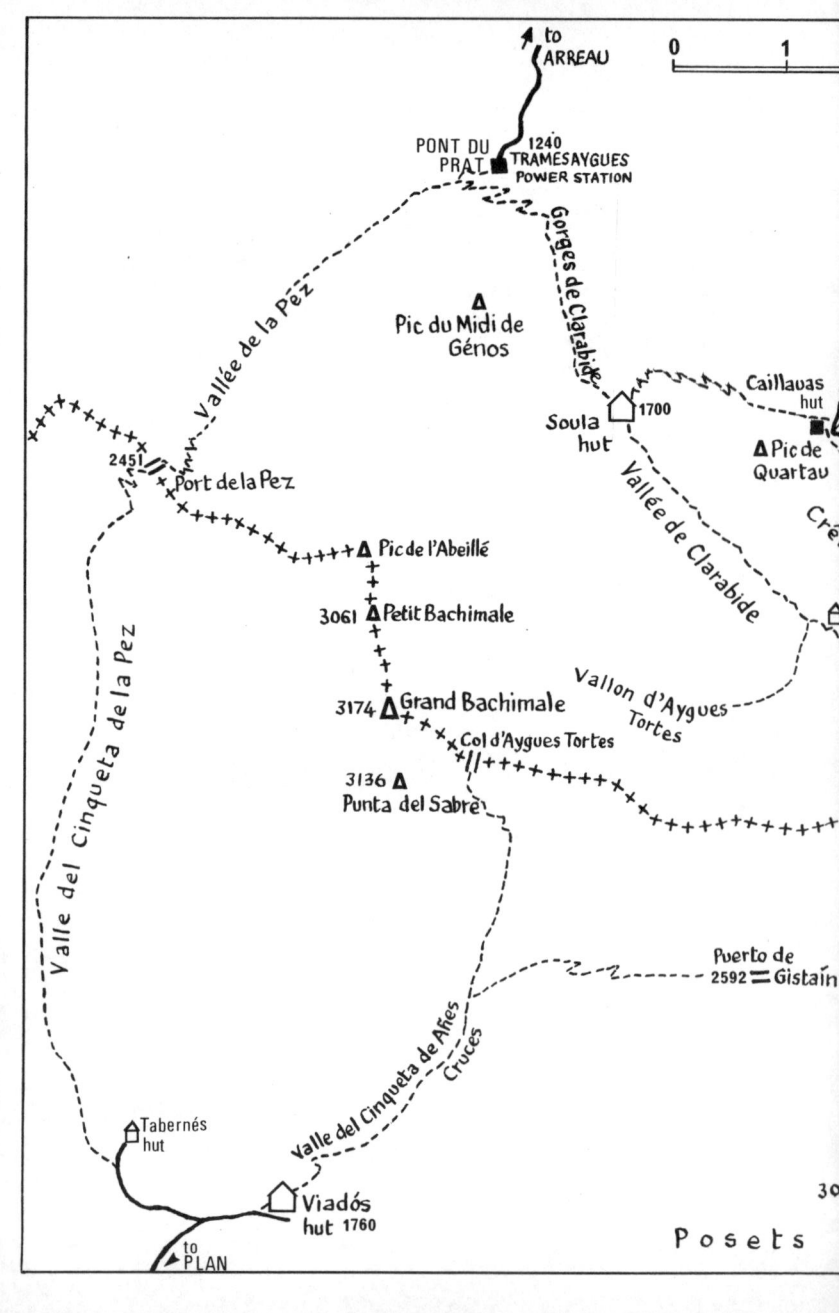

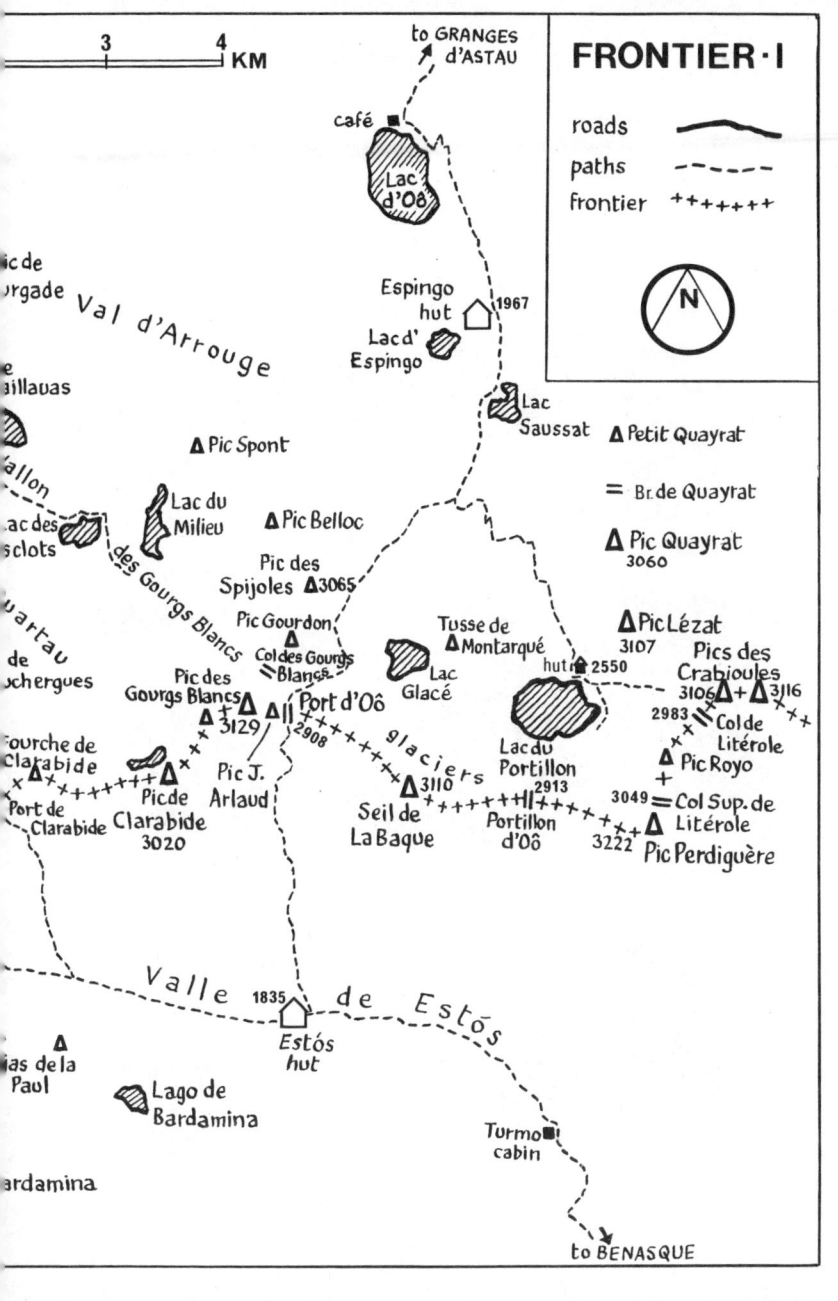

Frontier Ridge with the Seil de la Baque and Pic des Gourgs Blancs from the Portillon d'Oô.

Frontier · II

PIC DE MAUPAS TO THE SOMMET DE L'ESCALETTE

Maps: IGN 50m. n.1848. IGN/RP 50m. n.5. EA 25m. n.206, 207.

From the Pic des Crabioules the frontier, punctuated by a series of summits, falls gradually in height as it runs eastward to the Garonne gap. Towards the eastern end is the Port de Venasque, the main gateway to the Maladeta massif from France. N of the frontier there are no peaks of any consequence.

Luchon is the centre from which this area is approached; the western part by a road running up the Lis (Lys) valley and the eastern part by a road in the Pique valley, which ends at the Hospice de France. There are 2 small huts in the area; the Maupas and the Venasque; the latter is not very useful.

Refuge de Maupas 2430m

Start from roadhead in the Lis valley; café/carpark (1140m). Cross the stream by a footbridge and follow a path leading SE up into woods. This clear track heads up the Houradade valley above the L side of the stream. After about 3 km cross it near the Font de la Coume cabin (1714m) and take the path doubling back WNW; it gradually leaves a tributary stream and mounts gently through lightly wooded country and clearings until it approaches a pipe line, with a line of pylons above it, at Prat-Long (1890m).

From here the path rises steeply S in a long series of zigzags, keeping to the E side of the pipe line. About halfway up it passes a pumping station. At c.2400m the path reaches the pipe line. Cross it, and the hut is seen about 200m away on the NW side and near a tarn, the Lac d'Enfer (5h.).

PIC LÉZAT 3107m

Though the Portillon hut (Frontier I section, above) is right under the SW side of this striking peak, ascents from this side are quite difficult. The normal route goes out from the Maupas hut; a track leads round a narrow spur and contours SW into the Crabioules cirque with some loss of height; then take a cairned fork L, going higher to terrace pt.2457. Head straight across grass and scree due W in a rising traverse towards foot of the prominent Lézat NE spur. Turn this on the R(N) side and

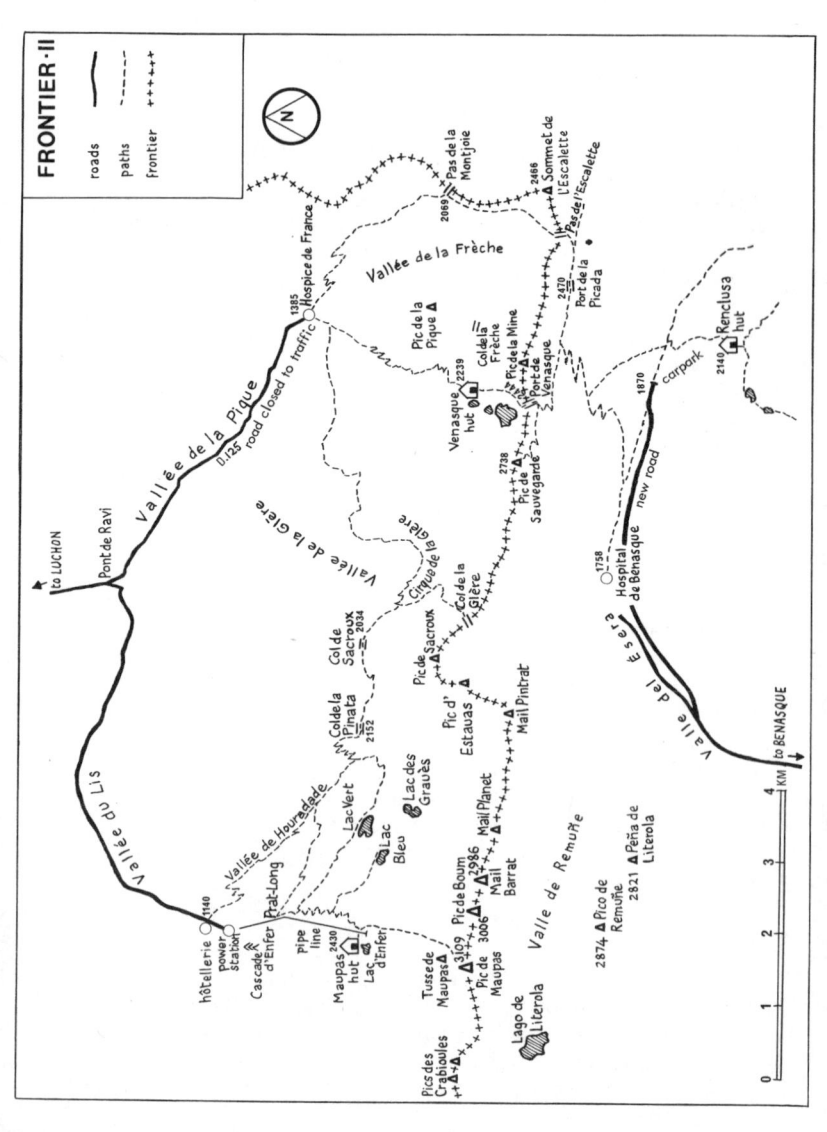

climb snow on the little Lézat glacier lying between the Lézat and the
Quayrat. An inlet on the L gives access to the NE spur above its terminal buttress. Ascend rocks by zigzag ledges/terraces to a gap in the
ridge of spur; from here go up onto a hanging scree/snow slope leading directly to the summit, PD (3 h.).

PIC DE MAUPAS 3109m

Normal Route. Grade, F. This peak was first climbed in 1825
by a military survey party under Lieutenants Peytier and Hossard, more
celebrated for their first ascent of the Balaitous in the Western Pyrenees. From the Maupas hut cross the pipe line and turn due S, following widely spaced cairns. Rise by a series of low rock terraces and
continue until the Tusse de Maupas, a minor summit (2900m) on the
NNE ridge of the Maupas, has been passed on your R. Bear R and
ascend the small snow covered Maupas glacier, keeping well to the R,
towards a small notch in the NNE ridge above the glacier's highest
point. Climb to this notch on easy rock, then follow cairns over a
jumble of large boulders to the summit (2 h.).

The view is interesting. To the E the Crabioules summit ridge is seen
in profile lengthwise, revealing the steepness of the N face (difficult
climbs on a mixture of compact schist and granite). S, under the Maupas, lies the Remuñe valley and beyond it a secondary ridge with 2
summits, the Pico de Remuñe and the Peña de Literola, both over 2800m.
To the SE, across the wide trough of the Ésera valley, rises the great
Maladeta massif.

Maupas rock climbs. There are 2 main routes on the N face,
reached by passing beneath the W side of the Tusse de Maupas. Both
are about 200m and graded TD, including artificial pitches. The S
face of the mountain rises abruptly from the Valle de Remuñe, a side
valley running W from the upper Ésera at a point 11 km N of Benasque.
Numerous routes have been opened on this face, graded D to ED, all of
about 300m.

PIC DE BOUM 3006m

On the frontier, one km E of the Maupas. A ridge falls from it to the
NE above the small glacier lying under the N side of the frontier ridge.

Normal Route. Grade, PD. From the Maupas hut, as for the Pic
de Maupas (see above) for about 30 min., then turn SE on a line towards the Pic de Boum, keeping this direction to the foot of the glacier.
Turn E along the base of the glacier and make for the lowest point of
the NE ridge at 2794m. Turn the foot of the ridge and climb the small

Pic de Maupas, Pic de Boum and the Lago de Literola from the Pic Perdiguère.

glacier lying between the Pic de Boum and the Mail Barrat, the next frontier summit only 400m to the E. Keep under the NE ridge. When nearing the highest point of the glacier, leave it and climb to the ridge by an obvious and fairly easy chimney. Continue up the ridge to the summit (3h.). The view is similar to that from the Maupas, except where the latter peak blocks the line of vision.

Mountain walk from the Lis valley to the Hospice de France

From the Lis roadhead, as for the Maupas hut (see above), up the valley of the Houradade, past the switchback (1714m), rising steadily to steeper zigzags leading to the Col de Pinata (2152m). Continue to the E, more or less on the level, and reach the Col de Sacroux (2034m), a little over one km from the Pinata. From here drop down into the broad Cirque de la Glère, following the path down and round its southern curve then its eastern side where it enters woods, the Bois de Bédourède. From here onward the broad path is obvious. After passing through a clearing it runs, almost on the level, through the larger Bois de Sajust and emerges into the valley leading down to the Hospice de France. Turn L down the Port de Venasque path to the Hospice, 10 min. away (7h.).

Hospice de France to the Renclusa hut (2140m) by the Port de Venasque (Portillon de Benasque, 2444m)

This is part of the route from Luchon to Benasque and is of great antiquity. Part of the Hospice de France at the roadhead in the Pique valley dates from the 11th century. This and the Hospital de Benasque in the upper Ésera valley were formerly staging posts for strings of pack mules trading between France and Spain. Today the route is the classic one from France to the Renclusa hut and the Maladeta massif.

From the Hospice de France ruins (1385m, large disused parking area, camping) the track runs S, rising gently at first then in a long series of zigzags to a plateau with a number of small lakes. To the SE is the Pic de la Mine (2708m) and the ridge of the Crête de la Pique running N from it, cut by the Col de la Frèche. To the R of the path, by the first lake, is the small Refuge de Venasque (2239m). The path continues under the W flank of the Pic de la Mine then rises in zigzags to the Port de Venasque, a V-shaped notch in the frontier ridge between the Pic de Sauvegarde (W) and the Pic de la Mine (E).

The greater part of the Maladeta massif, rising above the upper Ésera valley, is seen from the pass. The Pico de Aneto appears as a snow cone to the SSE, though the nearer Pico de la Maladeta seems at first sight to be the highest point on the long ridge.

From the pass the way leads down to the R for a short distance then swings L and continues under the S face of the Pic de la Mine along nearly level grass. Reach a small reedy tarn L of the path, turn R and descend into the valley by zigzags to where the main path continues SW. Fork L on a lesser path which fades as it nears the valley floor. Take a line S through scrub and isolated pines in the general direction of the Renclusa hut, which has been in sight since the Port de Venasque. Traces of a path. So reach the roadhead (1870m) of the C.139 which now comes all the way up the Benasque/Ésera valley to the Estan flats; parking, camping, signposts, etc. Continue up the big trail S for 40 min. to the hut (5h. from the Hospice de France).

PIC DE SAUVEGARDE   2738m

From the Port de Venasque (above) take a path W on the Sp. side and under the frontier ridge that continues easily up to this minor summit. Worthwhile for the view of the Maladeta massif, more extensive and finer than that from the col (50 min., 4h. from Hospice de France).

Circular mountain walk from Hospice de France

Take the path SE (continuing in the line of the road from Luchon), up the Frèche valley. After entering woods and climbing briefly, the path emerges on down-like slopes and continues SE gaining height gradually above the valley. Reach the frontier at the Pas de la Montjoie (2069m). Frontier stone n.335. The frontier here runs N-S. To the E the ground slopes away to the valley of the Rio Joueou, a Garonne tributary.

Turn R at the pass and follow a path S along the ridge towards the Sommet de l'Escalette (2466m) where the frontier makes a R-angle bend W. To the R, across the upper Frèche valley, rises the jagged Crête de la Pique. When about 500m from the Escalette, bear half R towards a saddle, the Pas de l'Escalette (2396m); cross this (frontier), turn R and descend slightly to join a path coming up from the Joueou valley. Take this path W for about 500m to the Port de la Picada (2470m). Cross this pass and continue W under the southern slopes of the Pic de la Mine to join the path coming from the Port de Venasque. Cross the latter into France and follow the trail N back to the Hospice de France (6h. for the round trip).

Posets massif

Maps: IGN sheets are entirely marginal and only EA 25m. n.205,206 cover all the area.

Noted for its terrible rock, the Posets massif, with the second highest summit of the Pyrenees, the Pico de Posets, covers a large area S of the frontier. It is bounded on the N by the Valle de Estós, on the E by the Ésera valley and on the W by the Cinqueta valley. The massif is divided into 2 parts. A northern section, with the 2 highest summits, the Posets and the Espadas, is separated by the Collado de Eriste from a southern section; the latter is somewhat less in height and has a large number of long radiating ridges. This section is rarely visited and it is fair to say that it is virtually unknown to most Pyrenean enthusiasts. Indeed the Posets massif as a whole until recent times has been one of the least frequented areas of the Pyrenees. Road improvements and the new, huge Estós hut have changed much of this.

There are 3 main huts: the Estós in the N, the Viadós in the Cinqueta valley (NW) and the Angel Orús in the SE. Several other forestry huts and shelters.

Refugio de Estós 1835m

From Benasque take the road N for 3km. After crossing the Cuera bridge turn sharp L up a short side road entering the beautiful Valle de Estós. Cars can be parked at the end of the road. The path from here keeps a short way above the E side of the stream; it turns NW, continues on the level then approaches the stream. Cross to the other side by a bridge and continue through sparse wood then open pasture where the path gradually moves away from the stream. The frontier ridge is seen to the NW with the southern slopes of the Perdiguero. The path nears the stream again and after passing a waterfall it descends, crosses a tributary stream and turns R, climbing beside the fall. So bear L and reach the Turmo shepherds' hut. Now cross the main stream and go along a little above it. The path rises over gentle grass slopes and through scattered pines; the hut is seen ahead, standing on a bluff on the N side of the stream ($3-3\frac{1}{2}$ h. from roadhead).

Note: For routes to this hut from France by the Port de Clarabide and the Port d'Oô, see Frontier I section.

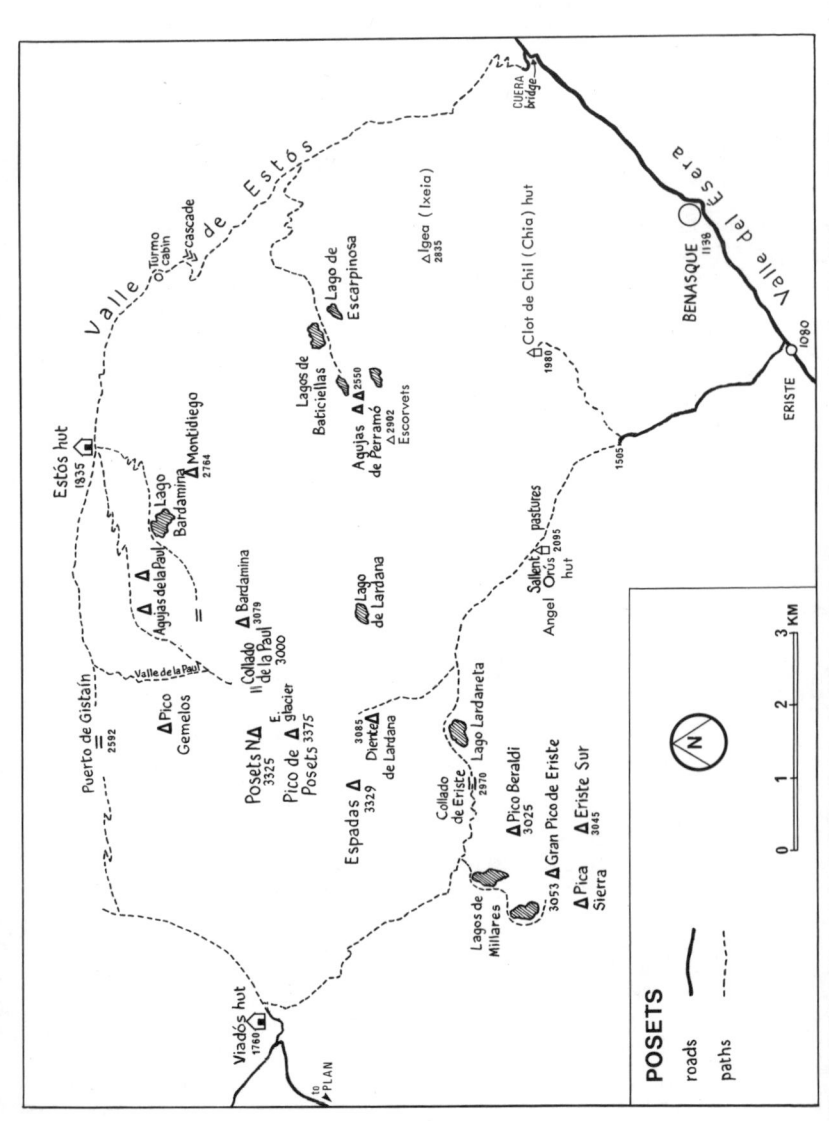

Refugio de Viadós 1760/1810m

Variable altitude, see entry under Frontier I section. From Salinas in the Cinca valley a good road runs up the Cinqueta valley through the village of Plan and above the hamlet of San Juan de Plan. In another 2km it swings back to climb to Gistaín (1422m). Where the road turns back a driveable track, signposted to the Viadós hut, leads N straight up the valley. After 8km the track heads NE for 4km, and after going over a bridge climbs E to end within 5min. walk of the hut above a collection of small buildings and barns.

The hut lies immediately to the W of the Pico de Posets. For a route to this hut from France by the Port de la Pez, see Frontier I section.

Viadós - Estós huts connection
over the Puerto de Gistaín (2592m)

From Viadós follow a track NE above the L side of the stream for some 3km, when the Gistaín saddle is seen to the E. Cross the stream before it is joined by a tributary coming down from the saddle, and ascend to the saddle by a path through boulders. The pass is in the ridge joining the Posets massif and the frontier ridge. On the other side descend steeply E over boulders and snow, then more gently, into the head of the Estós valley. When it appears keep to the N side of the stream and cross another one coming down from the Clarabide to the N. Wading may sometimes be necessary; cairn and path on the E side. From here follow a clear path on the N bank to the Estós hut (5h. hut to hut).

Refugio Angel Orús (Forcau hut) 2095m

Built in 1981 on the W headslopes of the Eriste valley, to serve ascents on the SE side of the Posets massif. The village of Eriste (1080m) in the Ésera valley is about 3km SW of Benasque. On the main road a little beyond the power station in Eriste a rough but driveable road ascends with zigzags into the Eriste valley and ends about 200m before the Espiantosa bridge (1505m). Attractive waterfall in a tributary stream above the bridge (8km). Cross the bridge and follow a good path on L side of stream, steeply at first then moderately to the Riberes barns (1815m). Cross a subsidiary stream and turn L(W) up a steep zigzagging track to the Forcau pastures where the hut is found a short way NW (2h. from bridge, 4h. all the way on foot from Eriste).

Refugio Clot de Chil 1980/1990m

Chia on EA map. Forestry hut under the SW side of the Tucas de Ixeia (Igea) group of rocky peaks which on the N side overlook the picturesque Perramó/Baticielles lake and forest hollows. At the forestry road terminus of the Eriste valley (see previous route), a clear track climbs

Angel Orús (Forcau) hut

steeply NE without possible error to the hut in 1¾h.

PICO DE POSETS   3375m

Also known as Punta de Llardana. First ascent, H. Halkett with P. Barrau and P. Redonnet, 6 August 1856. Several of the peaks in this area have more than one name; different valleys have their own names.

Estós Normal Route. Grade, F.

From the Estós hut drop down to the stream and cross it by a footbridge of logs. Turn E and follow a path on S side of stream; it soon slants obliquely up the slope of the valley away from the stream. Pass below the N face of the East Aguja de Paul (2685m). This is not a true needle, as the name implies, but rather a sharp-topped sugar loaf. Still rising, reach the foot of the West Aguja (Tuca) de Paul (2690m), also a sugar loaf; bear SW round it and enter the broad Valle de la Paul. A snow saddle will be seen at the head of this valley - the Collado de la Paul which bisects the W-E ridge joining the Posets North summit (3325m) with the Pico de Bardamina (3079m).

The path leads towards the centre of the valley without losing height; it then disappears. The route to the saddle remains obvious, going up snow then up the steep snow covered glacier below this saddle. With frozen snow, crampons come in very handy here. However, in recent years this 'glacier' has shrunk considerably and may vanish altogether. From the other side of the saddle (c.3050m) turn half R up the snow covered glacier lying below the E face of the Posets (also shrinking); follow the usual snow track steeply to the foot of a chimney in the E face. Climb it - neither steep nor difficult, but the rock is poor and care should be taken not to dislodge stones onto other parties. Wait for anyone ahead to clear the top of the chimney before starting up it. At the top emerge on the N ridge a short distance S of the N summit. Go along the wide ridge S to the main summit (6h.).

Very fine view. The Maladeta massif is about 20km to the E. To the N, the long line of the frontier peaks. Monte Perdido can be seen in the W and, in clear weather, the Balaitous as well. To the S is the neighbouring summit of the Espadas and the peaks of the southern part of the massif.

Note: The W side normal route by the Clot valley, W glacier and N summit, marked fairly accurately on the EA map, for a direct ascent from the Viadós hut, is a well known plod of 6-7h. over a vertical interval of 1600m. It is however recommended in descent (F+) for a simple traverse of the mountain.

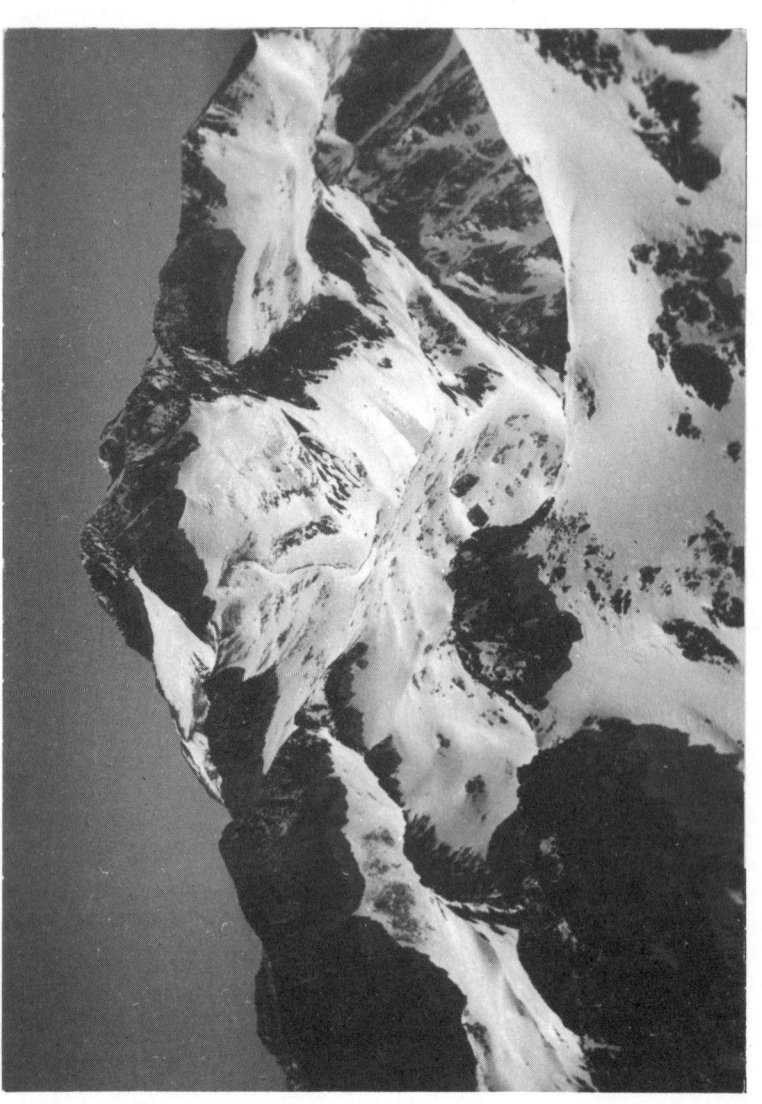

Pico de Posets, N and main tops, with Paul valley approach directly below, seen from NE.

Bardamina Route. Grade, F.

From the Estós hut go down to the stream and across the log footbridge. Ignore the path to the E and take the one leading straightahead that zigzags up the S slope of the valley. After gaining height the path bears half R over pasture then through pines and rocks, and reaches the Lago de Bardamina (2354m). Turn along the N shore then climb SW towards a saddle in the ridge running N from the Pico de Bardamina; this ridge forms the eastern crest of the Valle de la Paul. The 2 Agujas de Paul are to the N of the path but, as their southern flanks are gently sloping rather than abrupt, they are not particularly prominent.

On reaching the saddle descend gradually to the glacier at the head of the Valle de la Paul without losing much height, and join the usual route (above), coming up the valley (6h. from hut to summit).

Eriste (South-East) Route. Ungraded.

From the Angel Orús hut follow a track marked by cairns, rising NW across the Sallent pastures, passing the last barn (2265m), and higher up bearing R to cross the Llardaneta stream. Go up the R(N) side to small pools (2475m). Ahead is the Collado de Eriste (La Forqueta, 2970m), a saddle in the ridge joining the N and S sections of the Posets massif. To the R(N) another ridge curves SE from the Pico de Posets. About 600m below the summit this ridge throws out a secondary ridge due S, ending in the Diente de Llardana (3085m). The way to be follow lies up the short valley between these 2 ridges, where the Tuca Alta (2905m) stands on your R. Snow slopes merge into a gully. On approaching the junction of the 2 ridges, climb L to a saddle on the S ridge. Now follow ridge to the summit, keeping either to the crest or a little below on its W flank ($4\frac{3}{4}$h.).

Angel Orús hut to Viadós hut
by the Collado de Eriste (2970m)

As for the Posets SE route (above) to below snow slopes at c.2650m. From this point traverse and contour W to the Lago de Llardaneta, go round its N side then climb slopes of boulders and/or snow to the col, also called La Forqueta. Descend the other (NW) side in the bed of the long Millares valley, keeping to the R side of the stream; near the bottom change to the L side and a seasonal bridge over the Cinqueta stream enables the Viadós hut to be reached without going down to the Bordas bridge (5h. hut to hut).

GRAN PICO DE ERISTE 3053m

Also known as the Bagueñola, the highest summit of the southern section of the Posets massif. It marks the junction of 4 ridges. The NE

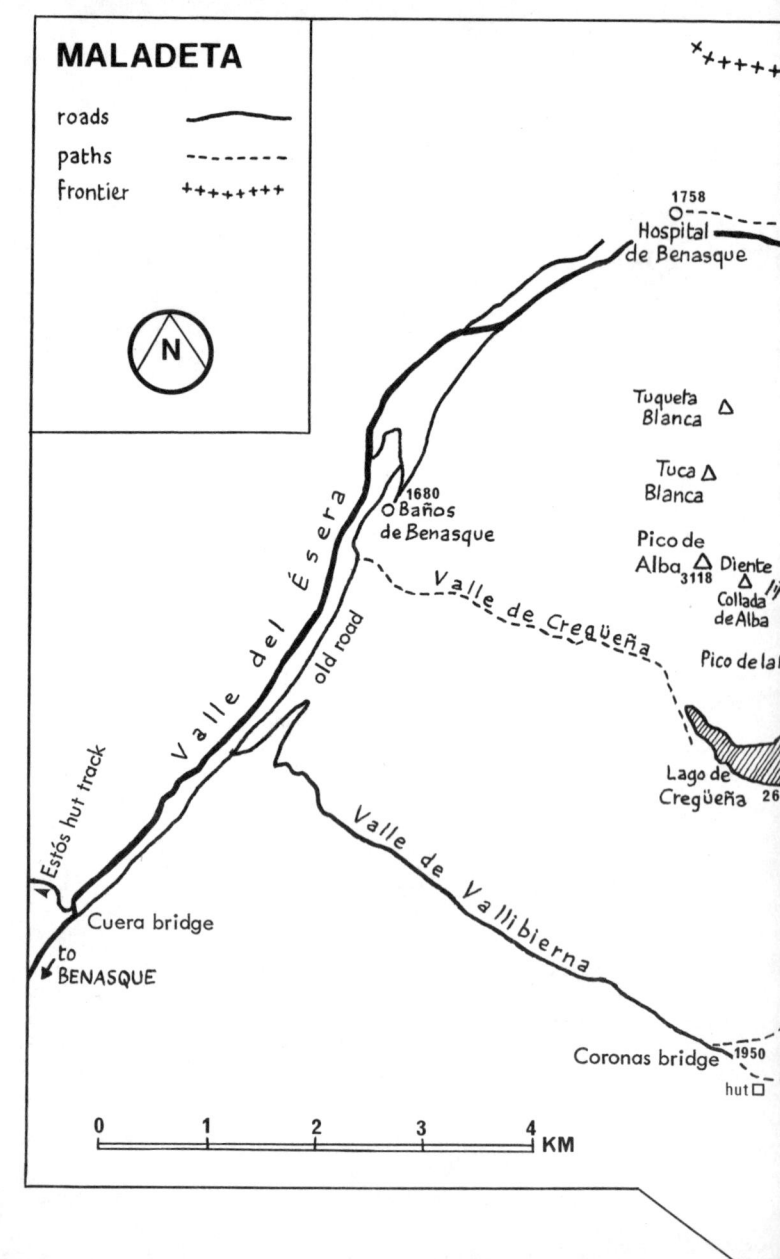

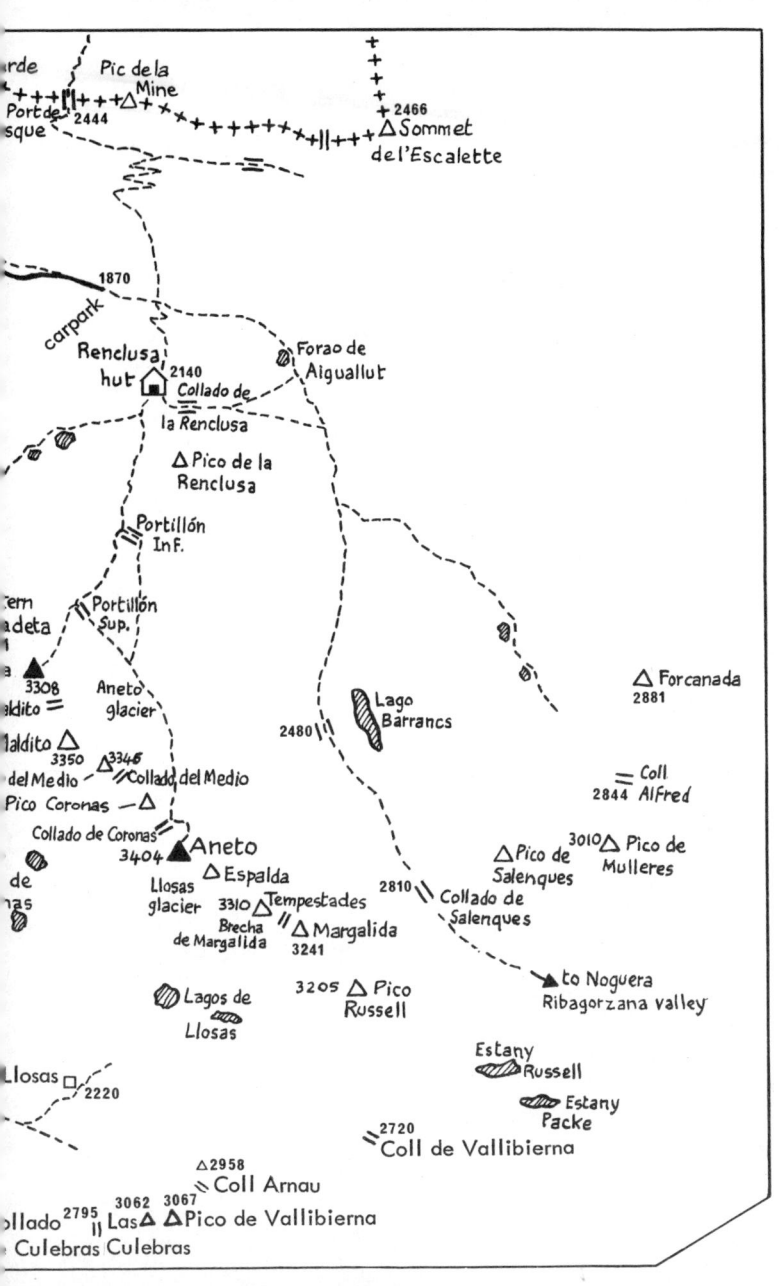

ridge, on which stands the Pico Beraldi or Eriste Norte (3025m), leads to the Collado de Eriste and the northern section of the massif. The SSE ridge rises up to the Eriste Sur (3045m), then it divides. The SW ridge divides at the Pica Sierra (2852m). There is also a short NW ridge.

By the Millares Lakes. Grade, PD. From the Viadós hut, reverse the previous route to a little above the point where a side stream joins the main stream from the S, at c.2240m. Somewhat higher, cross the main stream and slant up slopes to the lower Millares lake (ruined hut). Skirt round N end of the lake then climb more steeply SW to the upper lake (2525m). Follow round the W and S sides of this lake, then climb diagonally E to the NW ridge, aiming for a point short of where it joins with the summit. Ascend ridge to a snow filled gully leading to the summit ($5\frac{1}{2}$ h.).

Agujas de Perramó   2550m

The 2 main sections of the Posets massif offer no rock climbs but to the E of the northern section, in the angle formed by the Estós and Ésera valleys, lies a region of ridges, lakes and forests. It is connected with the massif by the ridge running eastwards from the Collado de la Paul and the Pico de Bardamina; the ridge then curves SE and divides to form a great cirque. This is the region of Baticiellas, Perramó and the Igea.

For the rock climber the needles known as the Agujas de Perramó are the chief attraction. They are reached by a path (signposted Baticiellas) that forks L from the trail up the Estós valley, about 3.5km from the C.139 road. The path winds up to the lower Escarpinosa tarn, situated in magnificently wooded country ($1\frac{1}{2}$ h. from the valley fork). The route then branches westward and climbs to the Baticiellas lakes. From the lower, and larger, lake turn SW to the upper lake. From here the foot of the N face of the needles is reached by climbing a slope of boulders and scree. Numerous routes have been worked out on this N face; several are graded TD or harder.

To reach the S face, where there are routes graded D, take the path from the lower Escarpinosa tarn that follows the stream SW to the upper tarn; then continue in the same direction to the higher Perramó tarn. Before reaching it, the needles will be seen to the W of the track. As the Estós hut is rather distant for routes on either side of the needles, camping beside one or other of the higher tarns is to be preferred.

The ridge of sugar loaf peaks running W-E above the Perramó lakes has other technical climbs to offer, though short. As summits, notably the Ixeia, or Igea (2835m), they are more readily approached from the other (S, or Eriste) side, where the Clot de Chil hut makes a good base.

Maladeta

Maps: EA 25m. n.207, 208.   IGN 25m. DB n.1848E.

The Maladeta massif proper consists of a ridge 7 km in length, lying NW to SE and to the E and S of the curving Ésera valley. This ridge, between the Pico de Alba (3118m) at the NW end and the Pico Russell (3205m) at the SE end, never falls below 3000m. Roughly in the centre of the ridge is the Pico de Aneto (3404m), the highest point of the Pyrenees. Every incident along the ridge is named, so there are at least 15 identifiable summits and almost as many cols or gaps.

A large number of lateral ridges extend from either side of the main ridge. On the NE slopes lie the Maladeta, Aneto, Barrancs and the Tempestades glaciers, all crevassed but normally well covered by snow in summer. There are also smaller glaciers under the SW side of the ridge.

To the E of the massif proper, but connected to it by a ridge cut by the Collado de Salenques (2810m), lies a secondary massif - the Mulleres group; this has a ridge running northwards to join the low frontier ridge at the Puerto de la Picada. To the SW of the main ridge, beyond the tail end at the Pico Russell, is the smaller Vallibierna group.

Discounting small, open forestry huts, the Maladeta massif is served by one hut only, the Renclusa, lying to the N of the Pico de la Maladeta.

Before the visit of Ramond in August 1787, the massif was unknown to travellers. He found that the local people knew only the lower slopes. He calls the range the 'Maladetta' or the 'Montagnes Maudites', the Accursed Mountains, assuming apparently that this was the equivalent of the word 'Maladetta', which is Italian and not Spanish. He explains that these mountains were "called, as is Mont Blanc, accursed, as they afford no pasturage for the cattle of the neighbouring valleys". Curiously, he also refers to an unidentified part of the range as the 'Malhetta', without realising that this was the true name.

The standard CEC guide to the region explains that the name Maladeta is a corruption of Mala Eta, a dialect form of Más Alta meaning, simply, the highest. Nevertheless the massif is still referred to in France as the Monts Maudits.

Refugio de la Renclusa   2140m

The route from the Hospice de France, over the Port de Venasque, is described in the section of the guide entitled Frontier II.

From Benasque (1138m) the new road NE in the Ésera valley bypasses all the former features connected by the old road on the other (E) side of the river. After the Cuera (Cubere) bridge, campsites, etc., the C.139 road follows the W side of the valley; new junction R for the Baths. It then gradually approaches the river, crosses it and bypasses the Hospital de Benasque ruins (1758m) to attain due E the Plan d'Estan (1870m) where it ends in parking places (18km from Benasque, taxi hire easy). From here by waymarked trail S to the hut in about 40 min.

Lago de Cregüeña   2656m

This lake site, the largest in the Maladeta area, lies in a deep cirque beneath the SW slopes of the Pico de la Maladeta and the long curving Aragüells - Estatats ridge. Start from the Cregüeña bridge (1468m) in the Ésera valley. From Benasque the quickest way to this point is along the new road to the Baths turning R; take this down across the river (campsite) to join the old road on the R, before the zigzags to the Baths. Go back along the old road for 1.5km, crossing the river twice, to the Cregüeña bridge. A clear path on the L side of the stream goes up ESE in woods, then up open ground to the lake in $2\frac{1}{2}$h. from bridge.

Vallibierna valley

About 8km long this valley gives access not only to the Vallibierna group but also to the SW flanks of the Maladeta summits and their supporting ridges. A driveable forestry track now goes all the way up the valley. From Benasque either follow the old road from the Cuera br. (4km) to the forestry track junction just after the Vallhiverna bridge (1369m), or reach the same spot by turning off the new road nearly 3km further on, where a lane R crosses the river to the old road at pt.1375.

The track climbs SE into the valley some distance above the stream and so reaches the Coronas bridge (1950m) over the tributary of that name, where a path branches NE to reach the Coronas cirque under the Pico de Aneto. Small parking places; small pastoral cabin beyond with no facilities; good camping spot.

THIRD WESTERN MALADETA   3185m

Normal Route. Grade, PD. On maps: Occidental 3. From the Renclusa hut follow the path SW on the L side of the stream for about 400m. Here a tributary joins it on its R side. Cross the main stream and find a path leading W up the L side of the tributary stream to the Renclusa tarn (2240m). This lies to the S and a little above the stream. From the tarn continue to a smaller tarn set among pines. Skirt round its NW side and ascend to a broad, flat rock terrace above a shallow valley to the R. At the end of the terrace, go down and cross a field of huge boulders lying at the end of an obvious glacier bed, rising to the S. Cairns mark the easiest way through the boulders as well as the start of the path on the other side.

Follow a path climbing more steeply; rocky outcrops. Higher up the path disappears. Go up towards the head of a kind of cirque formed by a spur of the Third W Maladeta to the L and a ridge from the Pico de Alba to the R. Cross snow patches and make for the saddle seen immediately to the R of the Third W Maladeta and to the L of the Diente de Alba, which is not seen as a definite summit from here but as one of a number of jagged points on the ridge. Climb the steep but short Glaciar de Alba to the saddle, the Collado de Alba (3075m). This is almost certainly the point reached by Ramond in 1787.

The summit of the Third Maladeta can be reached from the foot of the glacier but the rock is not good. The normal route is from the saddle, a direct scramble of about 100m up the ridge (bits of II). 4h.

PICO DE LA MALADETA 3308m

North Ridge. Grade, PD+. The long NNE (called N) ridge of the mountain ends in the Pico de la Renclusa (2700m), a minor summit above the Renclusa hut. The upper part of the ridge divides the Aneto and Maladeta glaciers. The ridge is also the watershed between the Atlantic and the Mediterranean. Paradoxically the waters from the western side flow into the Mediterranean, and those from the E flow into the Atlantic by way of the Garonne.

From the Renclusa hut follow the path SW and after c.100m turn L at a cairn and climb the well worn path to the N ridge, reaching it finally by a series of easy rock terraces. The path is marked by cairns in the upper part. It is the most frequented path in the whole massif, also being the approach for the normal route to the Aneto. There are a number of variant paths up the slope to the ridge, being shortcuts for the descent; but all lead to the same point on the ridge, a saddle known as the Portillón Inferior (2745m). From here the snow cone of the Pico de Aneto is first seen, rising from the broad Aneto glacier.

From the Port. Inf. the path follows along the ridge, or a little below the crest on the W side, over broken rock until it reaches a point above the Portillón Superior (2870m), a more obvious gap in the ridge. Before reaching this point, scramble down the W side of the ridge to the gap. Continue up the ridge by a short easy rockface. Above, the ridge broadens with flat slabs at first then broken rock. The Aneto glacier lies far below to the L but the Maladeta glacier on the R is only a few m below the ridge. Follow the crest to where it drops to the level of the Maladeta glacier and climb a steep pitch by a very narrow chimney back to the ridge crest; this is the only somewhat difficult part of the route and a rope is advisable. From the top of the chimney follow the ridge to the summit (5 h. from hut).

PICO DE ANETO 3404m

Fr. Nethou, the result of an error on the part of Henri Reboul, who correctly determined its height in 1822. The peak takes its name from the hamlet, Aneto, in the valley of the Noguera Ribagorzana to the E, though it is certainly not visible from there. As the highest point in the Pyrenees it attracts a very large number of visitors, most of whom make the ascent from the Renclusa hut by a fairly long but easy route. It was first climbed in July 1842 by Albert de Franqueville and Platon Chihachev from the W; Chihachev made the second ascent 4 days later by the Aneto glacier, the present normal route.

Normal (Northern) Route. Ungraded.

It is customary to make an early start. The whole hut is awakened by the hut keeper each morning at 4 o'clock with loud shouts of "Aneto, las cuatro !" This allows the rather tedious trudge across the glacier to be made before the snow softens and also ensures a return to the hut by mid afternoon.

From the Renclusa follow the Maladeta N ridge route (above) to the Portillón Superior. From here descend a gully on the E side of the ridge to snow slopes below. Follow the well trodden track in the snow, rising obliquely SE towards a saddle in the main ridge, the Collado Coronas to the NW of the Aneto. After a few hundred m the track reaches and continues up the snow covered glacier, which in normal summers presents no danger as all crevasses are safely covered. Late in the season, when crevasses may be open, the route from the foot of the Port. Sup. gully goes up under the E side of the N ridge of the Pico de la Maladeta then traverses the snow slopes under the main ridge, well above the normal track, as far as the Collado Coronas where they join. The slope to be traversed is fairly steep.

At the Collado Coronas (3198m) turn L to the foot of the summit snow cone and climb it. It is steep and if the snow is frozen, crampons will be useful. At the top of the cone (which is not the summit) bear R to a very narrow ridge of blocks leading to the actual summit. This is known as the Puente de Mahoma (Mahomet's Bridge), once considered difficult but easily crossed. The summit is crowned by a large aluminium cross and a statue of the Virgin del Pilar ($5\frac{1}{2}$ h. from hut).

Pico de Aneto from the Pico del Medio.

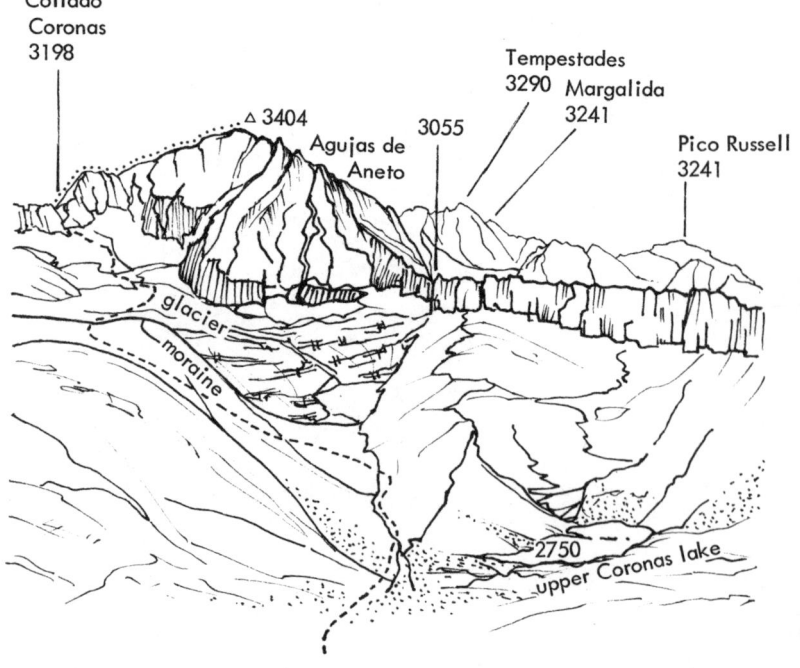

Naturally the view is extensive but it is not very interesting as all the
major peaks are far away and are often lost in a heat haze. The return
to the Renclusa can be varied a little by branching R at the edge of the
Aneto glacier, marked by boulders of the lateral moraine, and following a snow track direct to the foot of the gully leading up to the Portillón Inferior.

South - West Route. Ungraded.
At the Vallibierna roadhead (see above), a little beyond the bridge at
1950m, turn L up a path through woods on E side of the Coronas torrent.
It ascends some distance from the torrent, rising NNE to join it at a
small tarn (2220m). Pass along the E bank and bear R(ENE) to ascend
boulder slopes to a larger tarn (2635m). Go along its W side and work
up NNW to a third tarn (2725m). Move round the N side, heading E
and rising on a line above another tarn (2750m) over boulders and snow
to attain the foot of the little Coronas glacier situated in the angle between the main ridge and the Llosas ridge falling SW from Aneto. Keep
towards the L side of the glacier and climb steeply to the Collado Coronas (3198m), where the Renclusa route is joined (Coronas bridge to
summit, 5-6 h.).

Main Ridge Traverse. Grade, PD+.
From the Pico de la Maladeta to the Pico de Aneto. When consider-
ing this interesting ridge scramble, account must be taken of the time
needed to reach the first summit from the Renclusa hut, and to return
to the hut from the Aneto. The round trip is likely to take some 13 h.
Probably the finest mountaineering expedition of its class in the range.

From the summit of the Maladeta go down the S ridge to a point where
a cairn marks the head of a chimney on the E side of the ridge. Descend the chimney, turn R under the ridge and traverse a short steep snow
slope to rejoin the ridge at the Collado Maldito (3191m). About 30 min.
Do not get onto the crest of the ridge directly from the saddle; continue
beneath the ridge on the NE side; climb a gully of boulders then sur-
mount a gendarme. From here a slope leads to the top of the Pico Maldito, or Enmedio (3350m). From this top follow the ridge of boulders,
pass an isolated rock peaklet, Punta Astorg (3355m), and descend to a
gap - not too easy to negotiate. Climb back to the ridge and continue
to the next summit, the Pico del Medio (3346m).

From here pursue the crest without difficulty, and come down to the
snow/ice covered Collado del Medio (3255m); crossing this saddle can
be rather delicate. Onward to the next summit, Pico Coronas (3293m),
by the easy ridge, but the next descent to the Collado Coronas saddle
(3198m) is a little tricky. While the normal route from here to Aneto
is by the snow cone (see above), the ridge can also be followed.

Maladeta massif seen from the summit of the Pico de Posets (19th century engraving).

The ridge is steep and the rock is poor. So this is perhaps the most
difficult section of the whole traverse and care should be taken. The
ridge leads to the top of the snow cone from where the summit of the
Aneto is attained by the short Puente de Mahoma of the normal way
(summit to summit, 5-6h.).

The route may be shortened by leaving the ridge at the Collado del
Medio and dropping down a steep snow slope to the Aneto glacier,
where the normal route from the Renclusa hut is joined. There is
usually a bergschrund to be crossed beneath the Medio saddle but it
is unlikely to give any trouble. The rope is not necessary all along
the traverse but it is required for the more difficult passages.

Main Ridge SE Continuation.

The Espalda (Shoulder) of the Aneto (3350m), about 300m SE of the
main summit, can be reached without difficulty. Continuation by the
fine rock crest to the Pico de Tempestades (3290m), across the Brecha
de Tempestades (3202m), is complicated and includes pitches graded
III+ and IV; for experienced climbers only. The Tempestades and the
remaining 2 summits, the Margalida (3241m) and the Pico Russell
(3205m), can be reached by other routes, all long. The only direct
route to the Tempestades is graded D, with pitches up to IV+. There
is also no easy direct route to the Margalida.

PICO DE TEMPESTADES 3290m

Normal (South Side) Route. Grade, F. A satellite point is
awarded 3310m. From the Vallibierna roadhead (see above) cross the
Coronas bridge (1950m) and follow the track above the N side of the
Llosas stream for 700m distance to a fork. Go up the L branch through
a trench to the Llosas forestry cabin (2220m), close to the Llosas stream
again. The track heads NE above the stream and eventually crosses it
just below the larger Llosas tarn (2493m). Skirt R round S side of tarn
and follow the infall stream to upper tarn (2540m). At the inner end of
this turn L and climb N towards the foot of the Tempestades SSW ridge.
Bear R and ascend parallel to this ridge, up a steep slope of boulders,
slabs and snow towards a saddle, the Brecha Margalida (not marked on
map), between the Tempestades and the Margalida. On reaching the
saddle turn L along the main ridge over large blocks to the summit not
far away (4h. from Coronas bridge).

PICO MARGALIDA 3241m

As for the Tempestades (above) to the Brecha Margalida. Here turn R
along the ridge, keeping a little below the crest on the S side (4h.).

Margalida rock climbs.

The Maladeta massif as a whole is deficient in rock climbs of quality. In addition to the direct route to the Tempestades referred to above, there are 2 climbs leading directly to the Margalida summit; both are graded AD/D, according to the exact line taken. The N face, about 300m, is started from the Tempestades glacier. The long E (Salenques) ridge with pitches of II to III+ stretches from the Collado de Salenques (2810m); it is a classic rock climb. The approach from the Renclusa hut to the foot of either climb is long but not without interest.

Renclusa hut to the Collado de Salenques   2810m

First go down the Ésera valley path and turn R. Follow a path that rises gently and bears R to a slight saddle. Go over this and continue across grass as far as a broad and deep pit, the Forao de Aiguallut. This pit is a curiosity; a stream flows into it from the S but it has no immediately apparent outlet. There is, however, an outlet under the E wall, and through this the stream flows underground ENE for over 3km; it reappears at the Güells del Joeu and continues on down to the Garonne valley. The stream originates from the Aneto glacier, which is therefore one of the sources of the Garonne.

From this pit continue S up the valley, passing, on the R, the fine Aiguallut cascade above which the Aneto can be seen; 45 min. from the hut.

This point can be reached also from the Renclusa by a more direct way. Climb eastward from behind the hut and proceed alongside a small stream to the Collado de la Renclusa (2270m), a low wooded pass N of the Pico de la Renclusa on the Maladeta N ridge. On reaching a fork in the path below the pass on the E side, take the L branch to the Aiguallut cascade or the R branch to a point in the valley about one km S of it.

From here climb S beside the R side of a stream and cross a tributary coming from the Aneto glacier. Bear R then L and continue southwards to a fork in the valley. The L fork leads up to the Estany de Barrancs; the R to the Colladeta Barrancs. Take the R-hand fork and climb to the little saddle (2480m). Cross it and continue S with the slopes beneath the Barrancs and Tempestades glaciers on the R(W). Climb a long slope of boulders and snow to the Collado de Salenques. From here a ridge rises eastward to the Pico de Salenques; to the W is the Salenques ridge leading up to the Margalida (4-5h. from hut).

From the pass a path runs SE for about 8km to the road in the Noguera Ribagorzana valley, joining it about 3.5km S of the Viella tunnel. The walking is very rough.

MULLERES GROUP

This group lies to the E of the main Maladeta massif, separated from it by the Aiguallut and Barrancs valleys and by the Collado de Salenques. Well to the E of the group lies the Noguera Ribagorzana valley. The main summits are the Pico de Mulleres (3010m), the Pico de Salenques (2996m) and the Pico de la Forcanada (2881m), forming a central knot and throwing out ridges with minor summits. The 3 principal summits can be reached from the Renclusa hut by fairly long approaches, or from the E by equally long walks from either end of the Viella tunnel. Of these peaks the Forcanada is the most attractive.

PICO DE LA FORCANADA 2881m

From the Renclusa. Grade, PD. A forked summit clearly visible on the SE skyline from the Port de Venasque. From the hut reach the Forao de Aiguallut by one of the 2 routes to the Collado de Salenques (see above). Follow L side of the stream S for about 500m to where another stream joins it. Follow latter on L side until it turns to the SE, then cross it. Go along the R side, climbing slightly, and trend S into the Escaleta valley. The Forcanada stands above the eastern slopes of the valley, and the Mulleres and Salenques peaks at its head.

Ascend the valley, passing several small tarns. Above the last tarn, at c.2670m, climb diagonally SE up slopes of boulders to a saddle on the ridge between the Forcanada and the Mulleres; Coll Alfred (2844/9m), named after the French poet Alfred Tonnellé, who made the first ascent of the Forcanada in 1858. A more direct, steeper way to the col goes up almost due S from the tarn at 2460m.

The ridge ahead is not practicable. Cross the saddle, turn L and descend beneath the ridge on slopes of boulders; reascend to the ridge at a second saddle (2795m) S of the S summit (2875m). Traverse the latter top into the fork between it and the main N top, which is reached by a gully (5h. from hut).

Note: There is a route graded D up the very steep snow/ice gully of about 400m rising on the NW side to the saddle S of the S summit.

VALLIBIERNA GROUP

Peaks standing at the end of the Vallibierna valley, on a prolongation of the Maladeta ridge at its SE end. Beyond the Pico Russell the ridge drops to the Coll de Vallibierna (2720m) and curves SW and W to rise to the Pico Vallibierna and the Pico de las Culebras. The name Culebras means serpents and is taken from the swirling, contorted strata seen exposed on the peak's face. First ascents by Charles Packe in 1864 and by Russell in 1865.

PICO DE VALLIBIERNA   3067m

North-West Side. Normal route, grade, F. From the Coronas br. roadhead (1950m) in the Vallibierna valley (qv), follow the track E on the N side of the Llosas stream for about one km. Then turn R and cross the stream by a log bridge to begin the long even climb that rises to a broad saddle, the Coll Arnau (not marked on map), seen to the L(N) of the summit. Ascend in a depression called the Canal de Vallibierna, on the R of a long spur coming down from the L end of the saddle, pt.2958. The headslope becomes steep and rocky beneath the saddle, and is partly snow covered. Go up to the lowest point, c.2900m. Alternatively, a 200m gully to the R of the saddle can be climbed without difficulty. From the saddle ascend the crest S, passing the head of the gully, and turning 90° to the W so reach the summit ($3\frac{1}{4}$ h. from Coronas bridge).

PICO DE LAS CULEBRAS   3062m

Barely 200m distance W of the main Vallibierna top; the linking ridge is cut by a gap some 10m deep. In crossing this gap, the ridge becomes a knife edge known as the Paso de Caballo, which is often taken by sitting astride the edge, though it is possible to walk/balance along it to get to the Culebras summit, I+ (15 min.).

North-West Ridge. Grade, PD+. As for the Vallibierna route to where the Culebras barranco splits off from the Canal de Vallibierna. The ridge develops between the 2 depressions. Go up to the foot of it and climb the crest with pitches of II/III in the upper part, opposite the contorted rockface on your L. Finish by terraces and ledges of good rock at the summit (4h.). A feasible descent can be made by the twisting W ridge to the Collado de Culebras (2795m), then down the Culebras barranco to rejoin the approach route.

Encantados - Aigües Tortes - Sant Maurici

Maps: EA 40m. n.214, 228. 25m. n.208, 209, 210, 215. FEM 50m. Pirineos. IGN 50m. n.1948. IGN/RP 50m. n.6 (only editions dated 1985 or later). Warning: all mapping is still bad, especially the new RP one.

This very extensive area in Catalonia lies to the E of the upper Noguera Ribagorzana valley, to the S of the valley of the Garona de Ruda and to the W of the Noguera Pallaresa valley.

The first explorer of this region, though only of the western part, was Charles Packe, who in 1867 climbed one of the Besiberri peaks. Henry Russell wrote: "At that time the topography of these lost regions was veiled in such mystery - there was confusion about the names of the peaks and even of their position - that Packe himself might have had difficulty in explaining his route of ascent. Now, alas, we shall never know". Russell climbed one of the Besiberri peaks, the Pic de Avellaners (which he calls Besiberri West), in 1869 but the remainder of the region remained unknown even to him.

It is a very attractive area of lakes, woods, ridges and peaks with a lot of splendid, rough walking country, good scrambling and climbing of quality and some difficulty. The topography of the region is indeed chaotic. There is a high central area with the Punta Alta and the Gran Tuc de Colomers, and there are other high areas only loosely connected with it. To the NW is the long Besiberri - Serra de Tumeneja ridge; to the N the Serra de Saboredo; and to the SE, a long horseshoe of ridges round the Monestero valley, stretching from the Subenuix to the Encantats. The latter is the best known peak in an area still imperfectly known except to Catalan climbers and walkers.

There are a large number of huts, most of them small and with the minimum of facilities. Provisions for several days and cooking appliances are essential.

In recent years many of the larger lakes have been dammed by the electricity authority. This has resulted in the building of many access roads of varying quality; it has also reduced the time formerly needed to enter some of the more interesting parts of the region. For an outstanding modern evocation of the Encantados, see The Enchanted Mountains by Robin Fedden (John Murray, London, 1962).

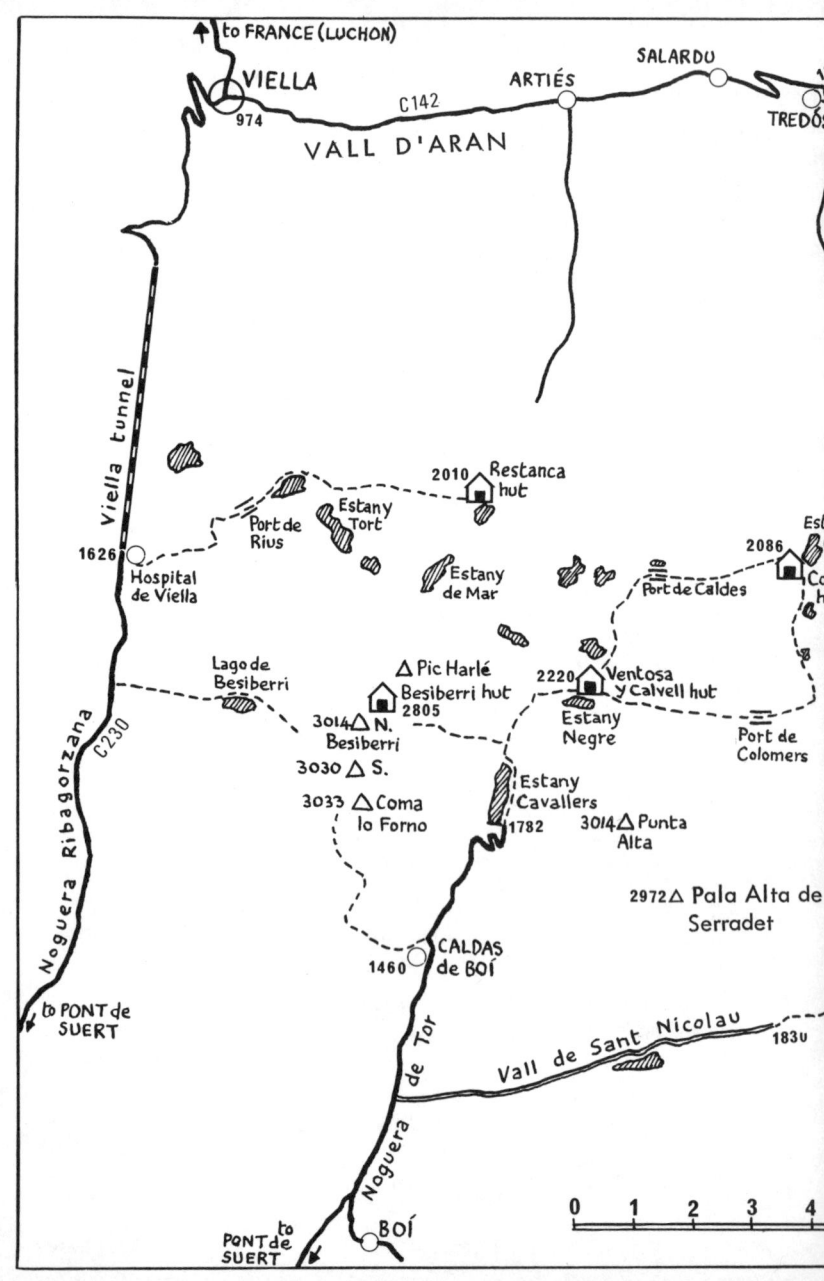

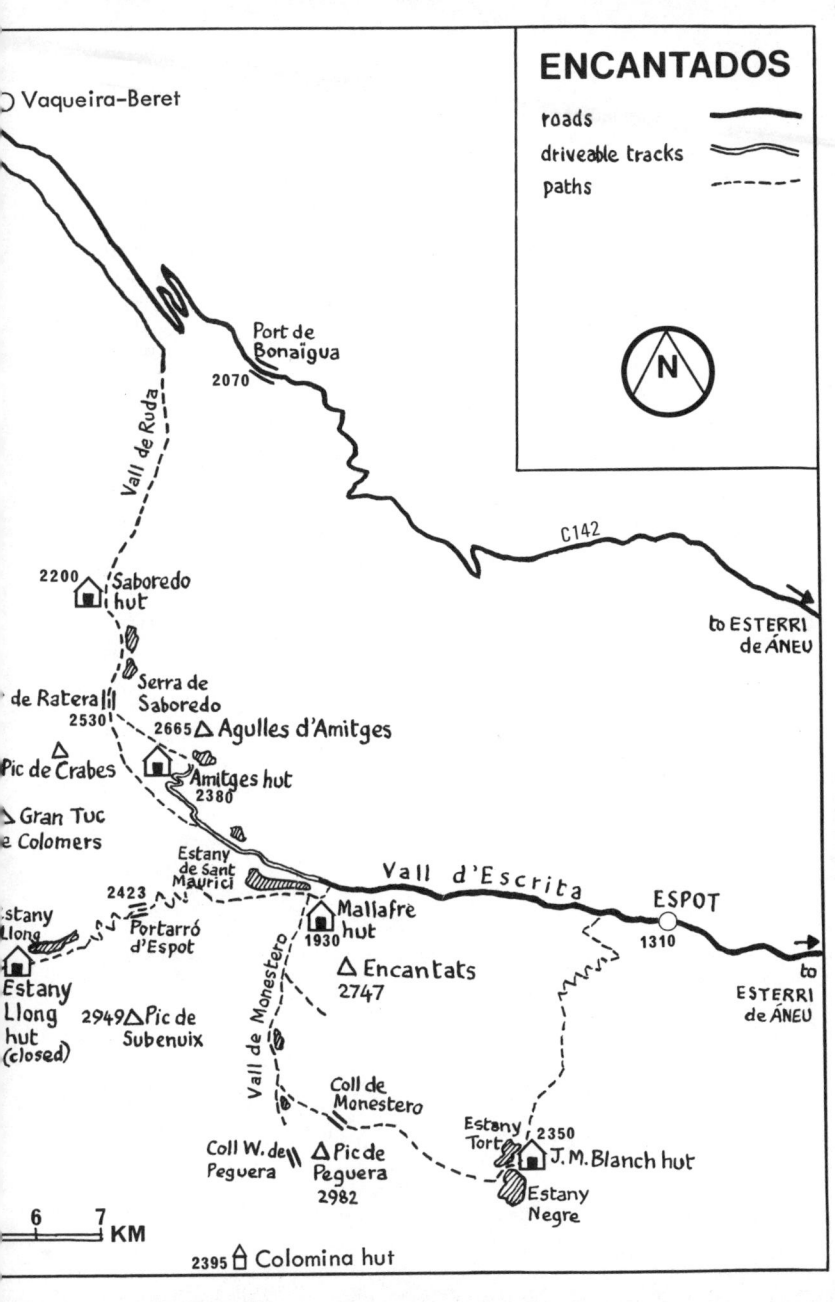

BESIBERRI RIDGE

This N-S ridge stands above the eastern slopes of the upper Noguera Ribagorzana valley. The highest point, also the highest point of the whole area, is the Coma lo Forno (3033m) at its southern end. Other summits are the Besiberri Sud (3030m), Besiberri del Mig or Central (3003m) and Besiberri Nord (3014m). From this last summit the ridge curves to the NE with the Pic Harlé, Pa de Sucre and Tumeneja N. The Besiberri biv. hut is situated a few m below the ridge crest to the E, between the Nord and the Pic Harlé.

COMA LO FORNO 3033m

From South. Grade, PD. From Caldas de Boí (1460m) in the valley of the Noguera de Tor, follow the road N for about 500m to where it crosses to the W bank of the stream. Leave the road by a path to L that turns back and climbs through woods above the Caldas de Boí hotels before curving into a valley above the N bank of the Sallent torrent. Continue for about one km and just below a confluence of streams (1990m, campsite) bear half R (N) and climb the side of the valley. Higher up work L and traverse the slope horizontally, turning the long ridge extending S from the Coma lo Forno. Continue N and above the E side of the Gémena de Baix lake (known to be sometimes dry in the past).

Further N circle above the E side of the Gémena de Dalt lake then more steeply to the higher of 2 small tarns, the Estany Gelats (2495m). From here climb below the Coma lo Forno S ridge to a saddle, the Colladeta d'Avellaners. Ascend steeply to this saddle over broken rock and snow; shortly before reaching it, turn R and climb a gully of about 100m to reach a point on the ridge a little N of the summit. This gully is subject to stonefall and the rock is rather poor; so care should be taken. From the head of the gully turn R along the ridge to summit (4-5h. from Caldas de Boí).

Very fine view, with the Maladeta massif to the W and the whole of the Encantados region to the E.

BESIBERRI NORD 3014m

Normal Route. Grade, PD. From Caldas de Boí (1460m) take the road to the high Cavallers dam at head of the valley (car park at E end of dam, 1782m). A good path from here goes along the E bank of the lake and on up to the flat expanse of the Riu Malo pastures, camping (1840m). Turn L and cross the main stream, the Riuet del Negre, by a log bridge. The Riu Malo stream is then met; this stream flows down an obvious valley that opens to the W, rising to the foot of the Besiberri ridge. Cross the Riu Malo to its N side; from here cairns mark the route over grass slopes to an increasingly clear path. Follow this, on the R side of the Riu Malo through a gorge. Pass a point where a side stream joins the Riu Malo from the SW (2220m) and continue to rise and reach a second gorge. Here it is best to move on to rocks in the torrent for a short distance to avoid a difficult stretch under cliffs. Return to the path on the N side and climb to the half-frozen Riu Malo tarn (2450m). From this point the Besiberri Nord is seen clearly. So too is the Besiberri hut, on the skyline to the NW, looking deceptively close.

From the tarn trend a little L and climb over boulders and snow on the L of a broad spur. Having turned this, bear half R and climb (traces of path) by steep schist slopes to the main ridge and reach it near pt.2832, between the Besiberri Nord and the hut (not visible from here).

Turn L and continue up the ridge over large boulders to a short rockface. Climb it; there are good holds. Continue along the ridge to the foot of the sharp rise to the summit. Climb this step by a series of pitches on the L of no particular difficulty and with good holds; so reach the top (6h. from the Cavallers dam).

Refuge-Bivouac Besiberri   IGC 2760m   FEEC 2805m
RP 2820m

Highest hut in the Pyrenees; it is normally used for making a complete traverse S of the Besiberri ridge. The hut can be reached directly from the Riu Malo tarn but the ground is difficult. The normal way is the same as that to the Besiberri Nord, as far as a little below pt.2832 on the ridge. Then work R from the track and traverse the slope across boulders to the hut, a distance of about 250m.

Refugi Joan Ventosa i Calvell   2220m

RP erroneously, 2150m. From the dam of the Cavallers lake at the Noguera de Tor valley roadhead (1782m), as for Besiberri N (above) to the Riu Malo pastures. Continue on E side of stream and cross it by the Palanca footbridge (1878m) about 2km from the dam. Now the path climbs slopes NE in broad sweeps, then bears E and passes above the N side of the Estany Negre (2127m, one of several tarns of this name in the region) and reaches the hut standing about 100m above the E end of the tarn (1¾h. from the dam roadhead). There is a very fine view of the Besiberri ridge to the W from the hut.

Besiberri Nord from Besiberri Sud.

Circular mountain walk from Ventosa i Calvell hut

Take the path leading N that, after passing a small tarn, reaches the southern end of the large Estany Travessani (2250m). Skirt the SE end of this lake, turn R and climb above it, then turn northwards and pass along the W bank of the Clot tarn. The Travessani needles (various scrambling and climbing routes) rise above the path to the E. Beyond the tarn bear NE and ascend steadily, trending E to the Port de Caldes (2550/2570m), a saddle in the Travessani ridge.

Cross the saddle and continue E for a little over 2km down to the Estany Major de Colomers (2085m). At the lake, turn R along its W bank to the new Colomers hut at the S end (EA mapping often shows only an older hut at the NW corner of the lake). From the S end, climb above the R side of an infall stream and reach a tarn. Cross a stream flowing into its SW corner and continue, rising above its E bank. This stream is punctuated by a series of 5 smaller tarns. At the fifth turn to the R and climb W to the Port de Colomers (2591m).

From this pass a track heads W, dropping gradually to the Ventosa hut, passing above the Culieto tarns; a distance of about 3.5km (5-6 h. for round trip).

Aigües Tortes - Sant Maurici W - E traverse

From the Noguero de Tor valley to Espot, presently designated a variation of GR11 and a curious alliance between the Fr. and Sp. park authorities. However, other Fr. GR trails elsewhere are being extended across the Pyrenees into Spain. Much of this one is along a more or less driveable track. Many excellent mountain excursions go off to the N and S from various points along this traverse.

Leave the road 2.5km S of Caldas de Boí and turn up a track (signpost) to the E through the Sant Nicolau valley. After 4km the track enters the National Park and its surface improves. Continuing past the Llebreta tarn the road climbs and ends after a further 4km. It is possible to drive as far as this point (1830m).

From the road end follow the N bank of the stream, curving to the NE then E. After some 3km cross the stream and follow the S side for a further 2km to the old Refugi d'Estany Llong (1985m), now closed and situated a little to the W of the lake of the same name. Pass along S shore of the lake, then climb by a series of zigzags to the Portarró d'Espot (2423m), a pass marking the watershed in this area. Now the path descends towards the Sant Maurici lake, seen below. As it approaches through woods, the track improves and, passing above the S side of the lake, winds down past the Mallafre hut (1930m) to join the motor road coming up the valley from Espot to the far side of the dam. Follow the road, with a good shortcut across a big double S-bend, for 7km to Espot. From the roadhead in the Sant Nicolau valley to Espot, about 5h.

Refugi d'Amitges 2380m

The Sant Maurici lake (1900m) is reached in 7km by a good motor road from Espot; taxi service. A rough continuation above N side of lake passes the ruin of a large building and continues the the Estany de Ratera. Very fine view of the twin peaks of the Encantats and the Monestero valley to the S. About 200m. beyond the Ratera lake the track reaches a smaller tarn to the L. A little further on a signpost on the L of the track marks the start of the direct route to the Port de Ratera and the Saboredo hut; this route is marked by small cairns. The main track continues NW and climbs by a series of broad zigzags to the large Amitges hut (1 h. from roadhead). Fine view of the Agulles (needles) d'Amitges above the larger of the Amitges lakes. It is possible to reach the hut from the Sant Maurici roadhead by Land Rover.

Refugi de Saboredo 2200m
by the Port de Ratera 2530m

From the Amitges hut the track continues for a few hundred m and ends between the Estany Petit and Estany Gran. At the last bend, leave the track by a faint path that runs along a narrow strip of land separating the Estany Petit and the Estany Mitja. Note: path shown on maps running along N side of the Estany Petit does not exist. Cross a sluice between the 2 tarns and continue. There are traces of a path but these soon disappear. Climb NW to a point from which the Port de Ratera can be seen to the NW, at the head of the Ratera valley between the great Saboredo ridge to the NE and the Tuc de Ratera to the W. To reach the pass, descend into the valley over long slopes of boulders to join the direct route coming up the Ratera valley (see Amitges, above). Head towards the pass, skirt the Estany del Port de Ratera on its E side and so reach the pass. About 1 h. from Amitges hut.

On the N side keep to the W bank of the stream when it appears. All maps for the ground hereabouts disagree entirely about the plot of paths. EA maps, which overlap, do not even agree with each other. On reaching the first large lake (contradictory map names for this and the next large lake) follow the W bank; also follow the same side of the next lake (2340m); on reaching the dam at its N end, bear half L and come down to the Saboredo hut. About $1\frac{1}{4}$ h. from the Port de Ratera, $2\frac{1}{4}$ h. from the Amitges hut, $3\frac{1}{4}$ h. from the Sant Maurici lake roadhead.

Serra de Saboredo.

The Saboredo hut can also be reached from the N by a good track up the Vall de Ruda from the main Viella - Port de Bonaigua road. The track leaves the road in the village of Tredos and follows the W bank of the stream in the bottom of the valley for about 8 km to a bridge at c.1650m where car drivers should halt (2 h. on foot). The track now goes up the valley S, on the E side of the stream and into a complicated cirque full of tarns in which the hut is found ($2\frac{1}{4}$ h. from bridge).

AGULLES D'AMITGES   2665m

Seen from the Amitges hut, these 2 fine needles are an obvious landmark, standing 750m to the N. The SW (apparent L) needle seems to be the higher although it is in fact a few m lower than the NE one. The SW needle has a number of rock routes graded D and TD on its S face. The other needle can be climbed by a relatively easy way from the N.

North-East Needle. Grade, PD. From the Amitges hut follow the road to its end. Go down the bank and cross the stream flowing from the Estany Petit to the Estany Gran. Turn L and follow a clear path curving round the foot of the ridge on which the needles stand, then climb N into a cirque formed by the Saboredo ridge and the Tuc de Saboredo; the path disappears. Go up the cirque and turn R on a slope of boulders towards a saddle between the Tuc and the needles. From this (W) side the needles are much less obvious. Just before the saddle is reached, bear R and ascend towards the base of the NE needle. Climb it by a series of gullies and terraces; there is a choice of fairly easy routes (2 h. from hut).

ELS ENCANTATS   S 2747m   N 2738m

A fine twin-peaked summit and the best known mountain in the district. It stands above pine woods to the SE of the Sant Maurici lake. The 2 tops are divided by a cleft to which a long gully rises from the foot of the mountain on the NW side. The rather formidable appearance of this gully is somewhat deceptive.

North Peak (Petit Encantat)

Central Gully. Grade, AD. 600m. For rock climbers; proper rope work, etc. needed. From the Sant Maurici lake dam roadhead, take the track S to the Ernest Mallafre hut (accommodation). Leave the track and drop down SE close by the hut to cross the stream. Now go up through the woods (path) to a clearing that angles up to the foot of the Central gully; keep L of a stream coming from it. A snow patch usually remains at the foot of the gully throughout summer. Tracks on

Els Encantats, divided by the Enforcadura and the Central gully.

the snow indicate the start of the route up the gully, which is seen to be less steep than it appears from a distance.

Climb broken rock and slabs on R side of gully; stonefall possible. Variable pitches of II/II+, all rather similar and with no particular problems. On reaching the Enforcadura gap (2697m) the crux is the last part above. It is possible from a few m down on the gully side to climb fairly directly above the gap, but this is harder than the usual way. From a point some 15-20m down the gully, climb out of it to the R by ledges leading back and up to a stance above the gap (II+). From here, turn a gendarme by climbing a short, narrow gully on L (III). At its head go L along a short, narrow ledge to the foot of a vertical pitch with rather small holds (IV). Above this climb a series of broad ledges then a narrow gully, from the top of which the summit is reached without further difficulty (3-4 h. from foot of Central gully). In descent, from the top of the grade IV pitch, 2 abseils are usual to re-enter the gully below the gap.

South Peak (Gran Encantat)

Normal Route. Grade, PD. As for the N peak route (above) to gap. Above, climb short steps (II) and ledges on R side of crest line to the top (3 h. from foot of Central gully).

Monestero Gully. Grade, PD. Traditional outward leg for the traverse of both summits. From the Mallafre hut proceed S on the main track for about 300m then branch L on a path marked "Monestero". Go along it in woods on the R side of the stream. After about one km the path reaches a clearing in which stands an altar-like wooden table with a cross (the latter may not be permanent). Bear half L and cross main stream. The path here is indistinct and there are several branches of the stream. Find a path on the S bank of a stream coming down a side valley, the Valleta Seca, and follow it for about one km to the foot of the narrow and very steep Monestero gully in the SW side of the S peak.

Cross the stream to the foot of the gully, which is a little over 400m high. While the gully is technically easy it is extremely laborious; the head is a saddle between the S peak and a shoulder (2710m) to the S of it. From here ascend bearing round to the R until you reach a crest below the summit, then go directly up short steps to the top. Traces of a path from the saddle (4 h. from hut).

Refugi J.M. Blanch   2350m

From the Sant Maurici lake roadhead and the Mallafre hut, as for the previous route up the Monestero valley as far as the table and cross. Continue due S, following the W bank of the stream. The path becomes

clear again. Reach a small tarn, the Estany Baix de Monestero, and
continue to a smaller tarn (3.5km from Sant Maurici). Cross the stream a little below the tarn and follow a line of cairns on the N side
of a stream flowing into the tarn from the SE. Go up a long slope of
boulders to the Coll de Monestero (2710m), between the Pic de Peguera (S) and Pic de Monestero (N).

Descend steeply from the pass and trend L under the ridge, then skirt
the N side of the Estany Gran de Peguera. Cross the stream flowing
from this tarn and follow its R bank past a smaller tarn. Re-cross the
stream and continue eastwards; pass between the Estany de la Coveta
to the N and the Estany de la Llastra to the S, then between 2 rounded points (2451, 2469) and reach the W shore of the large Estany
Negre. All mapping contradictory hereabouts.

Turn N along the lake to arrive at a dam; cross this and go L along
the E side of the smaller Estany Tort. The hut is seen on a spit of land
beside the lake (5h. from Sant Maurici).

Note: The hut can be reached from Espot by the electricity board road
suitable only for 4WD vehicles. On foot, $2\frac{1}{2}$h.

PIC DE PEGUERA   2982m

West Ridge. Grade, PD. The highest point in the National Park
proper. From the Sant Maurici lake follow the J.M.Blanch hut route
as far as the small tarn so indicated at 3.5km. Continue straight ahead
(S), cross the stream and pass a second small tarn. Cross a large zone
of boulders and climb a steep slope of grit and boulders, before coming
to a flatter area and the final slopes leading to the Coll West de Paguera (2726m). Across the saddle, go up under the W ridge and ascend
to the S summit (2923m). Now follow the ridge N to the N top with
several short bits of II (4h.).

Note: the NE ridge from the Coll de Monestero gives 50m. of grade
II below the summit. This is the usual route from the J.M. Blanch hut
(qv), about $2\frac{1}{2}$h.

PIC DE SUBENUIX   2949m

Seen with small but fine rockfaces along the E side of its N ridge, and
situated SW of the Sant Maurici lake. This worthwhile peak is easily
climbed (F) by its WSW ridge, or the S flank thereof, from the Estany
Llong site at the head of the Sant Nicolau valley (see W-E traverse of
park zone, above). This route is not directly accessible from the Sant
Maurici lake. The easiest way from here is by the road W to a vague
track forking WSW then S, going up past the Subenuix lake to climb a

gully to a small gap in the SE ridge, to the R of pt.2892. Then by a short scramble to the summit, F+ (3h.).

Appendix

MAPS

Since the previous edition of this guide entire series of maps have disappeared. Cuts in budgets and planning, and political rancour, have left the visitor with a less satisfactory and unsettled situation and future in the late 1980s. First to the Spanish side of the range.

In Spain, as before, government topographical mapping available to the public is old, out of date and quite difficult to find in local towns and villages. The military has a series of modern large scale maps designated 'military restricted' which is not sold to the public. Former series of French (IGN) mapping, including new issues since 1975 now withdrawn, extended some way S across the frontier, but in the last 5 years current IGN mapping has been cropped back so that only the minimum amount of Spanish terrain is shown consistent with meanderings in the frontier. This practice has been pursued to the ridiculous extremes of masking out 'excessive' display of the Spanish side with legends and tourist information.

The visitor is therefore confined to using the commercial EA series which now extends right across the Pyrenees Central zone as described in this vol. The scale of these maps is not consistent and varies from 40m. to 25m. (and some are 50m.). Inevitably these maps are somewhat crude and have several major shortcomings. Although contoured, they rarely show areas of rock and cliff, and forest zones are mostly absent. In other matters of detail, eg. paths and the distinction between pistes (forest tracks), jeep roads, and small metalled roads, vague approximations in category and direction on the ground soon become evident. Many paths used in the course of walks and ascents are not shown. A plethora of missing detail can be cited but a number of improvements can be detected from 1985.

In the late 1970s the FEM issued a single map in 50m. constructed from several IGC grid pattern sheets, extending E from the Aigües Tortes - Sant Maurici national park to the border with Andorra, and overprinted with tourist, walking and climbing information. It has been out of print for some years and is unlikely to reappear while the IGC mapping base remains so out of date.

France: The government agency IGN produces topographical mapping across the French side of the range. In 25m. scale the former park maps (PNP) have been replaced by another 4 sheets in the IGN Violet series (273, 274, 275, 276), laid down in a somewhat different pattern. These maps are due to be withdrawn (though still available in 1987), and in any case were never planned to be extended as a series covering areas outside the PNP. In 1985 a completely new plan for 25m. scale tourist maps (17 in all) was issued, none of which has appeared to date. This plan includes horizontal and upright formats of differing sizes and there are gaps between them, so that the mapping is not continuous. 3 maps based on the normal 25m. grid pattern in double sheet size, known as Double Blue, were issued for the extreme E (Mediterranean) end of the range between 1978-81, which seem to contradict the series scheme now awaited.

National grid pattern sheets in the 25m. scale are small (4 cover the area of each 50m. scale map) and are now quite out of date. Previous reference to these maps in the guide is now expunged.

Going down in scale the next series in 50m. comes firstly in a national grid pattern which has been subjected to simplified sheet numbering and some modification to ground shown along the frontier. These maps were always cited in the guide and remain so. The quality of these maps is superior to the newer RP ones (see below) but their updating has declined in order, no doubt, to thrust the RP mapping upon the public. As with all standard pattarn mapping, no overprinting of special information is given, but many purists will continue to prefer the clarity of this edition.

About 24 sheets in the 50m. grid pattern are needed to cover the Pyrenees along the Fr. side. In the early 1980s IGN collaborated with the RP organization to introduce a new series of 50m. scale maps, of much larger format, to extend along the range end to end.

This project has recently been completed in a set of 11 maps (10 if the superfluous double depth n.9 above n.8 is discounted). The formats are quite irregular, being square, horizontal or upright willy-nilly. Overlapping of sheets occurs to an extent up to 50%. What appears to be the final pattern only emerged in July 1986. Prior to this there had been 3 changes in the pattern plan since inception, and in some sheet number areas 2 maps of different extent and format exist. The earliest editions did not have the Spanish ground masked but now (1986) it is mostly vigorously obliterated. However, thanks to collaboration between Fr. and Sp. authorities over extending GR trails into Sp. territory, the RP sheet n.6, re-titled Couserans – Cap d'Aran – Pallars, in its latest version now includes virtually the whole of the Aigües Tortes – Sant Maurici national park.

A more serious retrograde step is a change in tonal values of inks used to print major features, eg. forests, easting relief shading, etc. The result, with a massive amount of visitor information overprinted (often too large) on the maps, is that many areas are grey toned and difficult to read. This applies to miniscule lettering and figures in particular, and in the clarity of contours. The problem varies from sheet to sheet. Bearing in mind that the base for this mapping is the fine 50m. grid pattern series (see above), and the amount of criticism already generated by the RP series, IGN will doubtless endeavour to rectify the poor apperance of these maps. Notwithstanding these comments the editors have decided to base all references in this edition of the guide, in so far as France is concerned, on the IGN/RP series.

In smaller scale again, the IGN 100m. Green series of tourist maps cover the Pyrenees in 4 sheets (69, 70, 71, 72). Except for n.69, very little ground in Spain is shown, and there is some deliberate masking in the other sheets. This is fairly good mapping (but not as good as the 100m. grid pattern series, ignored in this guide) and useful for general planning. For motoring the IGN 250m. Red series covers the Pyrenees in 2 sheets (113, 114). The W sheet (113) shows a lot of Sp. ground, the other rather less so. Beware about the perplexities of changes in road numbers and classification in France; in this respect Michelin uncontoured but equally good road maps can be more up to date. In all the foregoing mapping some old road numbers are retained, others are revised to new numbering, whereas others have a mixture of the two.

In summary, from W to E, the relevant mapping for the Pyrenees Central guide is as follows. All maps are obtainable from West Col Productions.

EA series:

40m.	204	Valle de Ordesa - Vignemale
25m.	205	Alto Cinca - Ordiceto - Bachimala
25m.	206	Posets - Benasque
25m.	207	La Maladeta - Aneto
25m.	208	La Ribagorça
25m.	209	Montardo - Aigües Tortes
25m.	210	Sant Maurici - Els Encantats
40m.	214	Pont de Suert - Escales
40m.	228	La Vall d'Aran
25m.	231	Cotiella - Peña Montañesa

FEM 50m. Pirineos (for Sp. nat. park area etc.). Out of print.

IGN 25m. Violet series:

275 Gavarnie-Néouvielle   276 Néouvielle-Vallée d'Aure

IGN 50m. grid pattern series:

1747	Campan	1848	Bagnères de Luchon
1748	Vielle-Aure	1948	Pic de Maubermé

IGN/RP 50m. series:

4 Bigorre   5 Luchon   6 Couserans (Aigües Tortes edition)

IGN 100m. Green series:

70 Pau-Bagnères de Luchon   71 St-Gaudens-Andorre

IGN 250m. Red series: 113 Pyrénées Occidentales

Supplementary map information

The reference above to the awaited new series of IGN tourist maps in 1/25,000 based on the DB (double blue) formats materialised with the release in 1987 of most of these sheets. As forecast, the formats and area covered by each map vary tremendously, but overlapping has been eliminated. Where Spanish terrain is shown, this is presented in faded monochrome with no updating. The erratic formats make 2 and sometimes 3 maps necessary over some areas covered by one RP map. The data and presentation is of the same superior standard and quality of the IGN/PNP sheets n.273-276 inclusive; these are now withdrawn even though retailer stocks may last throughout 1988.

An illogical feature of this series is that regular DB sheet areas off the national grid pattern do not appear to underlie the tourist versions, which are given similar (confusing) numbers. To date (January 1988) at least 4 regular DB sheets are needed to supplement areas not covered by DB tourist sheets. Altogether, an unsatisfactory sheet plan which will probably end up being totally revised and recast.

A summary of these new IGN 25m. DB scale tourist maps relevant to area sections of the West and Central guidebooks is as follows:

Pyrenees West

Larrau-Haute Soule 1447N, 1547W
Belagua-Ansó-Hecho 1447N, 1547W   Lescun 1547W
Aspe 1547W, 1547E   Ossau 1547E
Southern Limestone Range 1648E   Eaux-Bonnes 1547E
Balaitous 1547E, 1647E, 1648E   Marcadau 1647E, 1648E
Vignemale 1647E, 1648E
Gavarnie-Ordesa-Perdido 1648E, 1748W

Pyrenees Central

Estaubé-Pineta-Troumouse 1748W   Frontier I   1748E, 1848W
Néouvielle   1747W, 1747E, 1748W   Frontier II 1848W, 1848E
Vallée d'Aure   1748W, 1748E   Posets   1848E
Barrosa-Ordiceto-Suelza 1748W, 1748E   Maladeta   1848E

Areas not included are outside the sheet plan of this series. Areas in Spain may only be shown in small parts of particular maps. Category N are horizontal "slot" formats. Categories E and W vary from square to squat and regular upright formats. (In the Pyrenees East zone there are horizontal landscape formats, as well as N slot formats).

FOREIGN TECHNICAL PUBLICATIONS

Some 150 volumes in French, Spanish and Catalan have been issued in the last 15 years, for walking, trekking, touring, backpacking and climbing, inclusive of catalogue type publications (hut lists/accommodation, etc.). These are constantly changing, disappearing or coming up again in other forms.

In France the Ollivier series deals with serious technical climbs in about 12 vols - issued in French, Spanish or Catalan according to the area. In Spain numerous independent technical climbing guides are published in the native languages, notably the CEC series.

The Pyrenees High Level Route (HRP) is covered in one volume and is available in French, Catalan and English. The GR 10 low level way along the French side of the range comes in 5 vols inclusive of many variations, and is in French only.

There is a five-fold duplication in French guides for walkers over some areas of the Pyrenees. New GR touring routes and circular excursions are constantly being introduced by government and local agencies on the Fr. side, which merely aggravates and confuses the multiplicity of choice. A similar membrane of excursions can now also be seen to be forming on the Sp. side of the range.

Index

Abeillé, Pic de l' 63
Abetos, Los 16
Aiguallut fall 100
Aigües-Tortes 12, 103
Ainsa 59
Alba, Collado de 93
- Pico de 93
Alfred, Coll 101
Alta, Punta (Cotiella) 59
Alta, Punta (Encantados) 103
Amitges, Agulles d' 13, 110, 112
- hut 21, 110
Aneto, Pico de 12, 25, 26, 94
Angel Orús hut 20, 83
Aran, Vall d' 16, 21
Arbizon, L' 47
Aret, Pic d' 50
Arlaud, Pic Jean 68
Armeña hut 20, 55
Arreau 15, 48
Arriouère, Pic d' 50, 54
Arrouy, Mont 36
Arties 16
Aspin, Col d' 47
Aubert, Hourquette d' 42
Aulon gite 18
Avajan 15

Bachimale, Gd. 63
- Petit 63
Badet col 46
- Pic 46
Bagueñola 87
Baqueira-Beret 16
Barbaruens 20, 55
Bardamina, Pico de 85, 87
Barèges 25, 39, 42, 47
Barrosa, Pico de 52

Barroude hut 48
- Port de 52
- Wall 13, 36, 48
Bastan, Pic de 42
Batoua, Pic de 50
Benasque 16, 92
Beraldi, Pico 90
Besiberri biv. hut 20, 106, 107
- del Mig/Central 106
- Nord 106
- ridge 106
- Sud 106
Bielsa 16, 32
- Port de 49
- tunnel 14, 23, 49
Bigorre, Bagnères de 15, 47
- Pic du Midi de 47
Blanc, Petit Pic 37
Blanch hut 21, 114
Boi 17
Bonneu, Pic de 36
Bordères de Louron 15
Boum, Pic de 77
Bugarret col 45
Burbe, Portillon de 14, 23

Caballos, Paso de los 52
Cadéac 15
Caillauas hut 19, 65
Caldas de Boi 15, 17, 106, 109
Caldas, Port de 109
Campana de Cloutou hut 18, 42
Campbieil, Pic de 45
Camping 23
Canau, Port de la 36
Castejón de Sos 16, 60
Cauarère, Port de 50
Cavallers dam 106

123

Caving 14, 55
Ceresa 59, 60
Chinipro 37
Cilindro, Cuello de 33
Cinca valley 16
Cinqueta valley 16, 20
Clarabide valley 18
Clarabide, Fourche de 64
- Port de 64
Clot de Chil (Chia) hut 20, 83
Collubert saddle 59
Colomers hut 21, 109
Colmers, Gran Tuc de 103
- Port de 109
Colomina hut 21
Como lo Forno 106
Contade, Pic du 42
Coronas hut 92
Coronas, Collado 94, 97
- Las 59
- Pico 97
Cotiella 12-14, 20, 55
- Pico de 59
Crabioules, Pic des 13, 68
Cregüeña lake 92
Culebras, Collado de 102
- Pico de las 101, 102
Culfrèda, Pic de 50

Diente de Llardana 87

Encantados 12, 13, 20, 103
Encantats, Els 112-114
Enmedio, Pico 97
Equipment 23
Eriste 16, 83
- Collado de 87
- Gran Pico de 87
- Norte 90
- Sur 90
Escalette, Sommet de l' 80
Escrita valley 17
Ésera valley 16, 20, 92
Espade, Pic d' 46
Espingo hut 19, 66

Espot 17, 110, 115
Espot, Portarró d' 109
Espouy, Pico de 59
Estany Llong hut 21, 109
Estarvielle 15
Estaubé cirque 12, 17, 31
Estibe 42
Estós hut 20, 64, 65, 66, 81

Fabian 15, 48
Fauna 27
Feliú, San 60
Ferrera, Sierra 59
Flora 28
Forcanada, Pico de la 101
Forcarral, Pte. du 32
Forcau hut 20, 83
France, Hospice de 14, 16, 79
Fulsa, Punta 54

Garin 15
Garonne gap 12
- valley 14
Gèdre 31
Geology 13
Gerbats, Pic de 36, 37, 48
Gistain 83
- Puerto de 14, 83
Glaciers 24
Glère hut/hotel 18, 39
Gloriettes dam 31
Gourdon, Pic 65
Gourgs Blancs, Pic des 65
Granges d'Astau 66
- de Camoudiet 47
- de Lurgues 47
Guchen 18, 47

Harlé, Pic 106
Heid, Pic 37, 49
Hospice de Benasque 92
- de France 14, 16, 79
- de Rioumajou 15, 49, 54
Hourgade, Pic de 65

Igea group 83, 90
Ixeia group 83, 90

Juli Soler i Santalo chalet 21

Larboust valley 15
Lary, St. 15, 48
Laspuña 59, 60
Ledormeur, Pte. 63, 64
Lézat, Pic 75
Lis (Lys) valley 16, 19, 75, 79
Litérole, Col (Inf.) de 68
- Col Sup. de 71
Llong hut, Estany 21, 109
Llosas hut 99
Long, Pic 13, 45
Loudenvielle 15, 62
Luchon, Bagnères de 14-16

Madère, Port de 50
Mail Barrat 79
Maladeta general 12, 13, 25, 26, 91
Maladeta, Picos de la 92, 93, 97
Maldito, Pico 97
Mallafre hut 21, 109, 112
Margalida, Pico 99
Marie de Campan, Ste. 15
Maubic, Pic 45
Maupas hut 19, 75
Maupas, Pic de 13, 77
Méchant, Pic 46
Medio, Pico del 97
Midi de Bigorre, Pic du 47
Mine, Pic de la 79
Monestero, Coll de 115
Monfaucon 47
Mongie, La 15, 47
Montañesa, Peña 59
Montjoie, Pas de la 80
Moudang, Port du 49
- valley 49
Mountain rescue 24
Mulleres group 101
Munia, Col de la 35
- lakes 37
- Pic de la 35
Muria, Puerto de la 60

National parks 12
Néouvielle area 12, 13, 18, 39
Néouvielle, Pic de 42
Neuf de Pinède, Port 32
Noguera Ribagorzana 16
Noguera de Tor 17, 109

Ordiceto lake 52
Orédon hut/inn 18, 39, 42
Oô lake/inn 19, 66
Oô, Port d' 25, 66
- Portillon d' 71
Oule chalet/hotel 18
Ourdissétou, Port d' 50, 54

Packe hut 18, 39
Parzan 37
- Hospital de 49, 52
Paul, Agujas 85, 87
- valley 85
Peguera, Coll W de 115
- Pic de 115
Pène Blanque 36
Perdido, Monte 25, 33
Perdiguère, Pic 70
Perramó, Agujas de 13, 90
Peyresourde, Col de 15
Pez, Port de la 62
Piau-Engaly 48
Picada, Port de la 80
Pinata, Col de 79
Pinède, Pic de 32
Pineta cirque/lake 32
- valley 16
Pique valley 19, 75, 79
Plan 16, 83
Plan, Port de 50
Pont de Prat 32
- du Roi 14, 23
- de Suert 15
Portillon hut 19, 66
Posets massif 12-14, 81
Posets, Pico de 25, 26, 85
Pouchergues hut 19

Quarte-Termes, Pic des 42

125

Quayrat, Pic 13, 68

Ratera, Port de 110
- Tuc de 110
Redundo 59
Renclusa hut 20, 79, 91, 92
Renclusa, Collado de la 100
- Pico de la 93
Restanca hut 21
Rioumajou valley 49
- Hospice de 15, 49, 54
Robiñera 37
Royo, Pic 71
Russell, Pico 26, 99

Saboredo hut 21, 110, 112
Saboredo, Serra de 110, 112
Sabre, Punta del 64
Sacroux, Col de 79
Salardu 16, 21
Salenques, Collado de 100
- Pico de 100, 101
Salinas 16, 83
Sant Maurici area 12, 103
Sant Maurici lake 109, 110
Sauvegarde, Pic de 80
Saux valley 49
Schrader, Pic 63
Sède, Col de la 36, 37
Seil de la Baque 68
Señal de Viadós saddle 64
Serre-Mourène 36
Sierra, Pica 90
Soula hut 18, 63
Spijoles, Pic des 13, 70

Sucre, Pa de 106
Suelza, Punta 54

Tabernés hut 20, 63
Tempestades, Pico de 26, 99
Toudes, Pic des 46
Tourmalet, Col du 15, 47
Tourrat col 45
Tramesaygues 62
Travessani needles 109
Trigoniero hut 19, 49
- valley 19, 49, 54
Troumouse cirque 12, 15, 31, 35
- Pic de la 36, 48
Tuca Alta 87
Tuquerouye hut 17, 25, 26, 31
- (and Br.)
Turbón, El 12, 13, 60

Vallibierna, Coll de 101
- Pico de 101, 102
- valley 92
Vaqueira-Beret 16
Venasque hut 19, 79
Venasque, Port de 79
Ventosa i Calvell hut 21, 107, 109
Viadós hut 20, 62, 83
Viella tunnel 15, 16
Vielle-Aure gite 18
Vieux, Port 52
Vilas baths 60

Weather 13